About the Author

James Ray Ellerston, born in 1950, is a poet, historian, musician, father and husband who has traveled nine times to Europe, as well as western Canada and the United States including Alaska and Hawaii. He was a music educator for thirty-three years in Iowa, performing on violin and viola in community ensembles. He earned a B.A. from Central College (Pella, Iowa) in 1972, an M.S. in Education from Bemidji State University in 1976 and an additional B.A. in Management and Personnel from Buena Vista University in 1987.

James resides in Fort Dodge, Iowa and has spent part of each summer for the past fifty-nine years at his cabin on Ten Mile Lake near Hackensack, Minnesota. He married his editor and wife Shelley in 1978.

Poetry has a way of adding power to
words. Well done, I enjoy your work.
I love and read poetry more intensely
than anything else now, and I find
all the greats write more poetry
expressing "hard" themes rather than
"light". Those things through the ages
needed more exposure to show the nature
of mankind—I guess.

Raymond Schamel, October 9, 2015

Sand and Rock at Normandy 1944 (June 6th)

In the annals of history poets must forever teach
        what they felt when ordered to hit the beach;
And how for decades they misty-eyed up-tear
        for soldier friends long forgotten;
Now these are somehow anguished quick remembered,
        still held in cloudy places dear.

With true fierceness that June morning
        they assaulted bullets' rain and hail;
An armada of ships road the swelling sea
        to deliver an army ashore,
Fighting their way landward
        in storm-driven surf blown by gale;
Under smoke clouds men were shot up, split open,
        intestines spilt on sand and rock floor,
Men cried out for their mothers,
        prayed to their God for courage and more;
Stars and crosses now mark those who died there,
        turning sea water red in the gore;
For sacrificed youth and cut-off lives
        we give thanksgiving evermore;
Yet these men in old age tell of muscled youth
        and defiance in remembered lore;
It is the future work of distant poets
        to make real these soldiers still troubling feelings;
It is the job of statesmen to make peace
        and with historic memories promote world healing;
To make a better world these men on D-Day
        let blood of their 'greatest generation' outpour.

In the annals of history poets must forever teach
        what they felt when ordered to hit the beach;
And how for decades they misty-eyed up-tear
        for soldier friends long forgotten;
Now these are somehow anguished quick remembered,
        still held in cloudy places dear.

James R. Ellerston
June 5, 2014

Events Of Time

Through Life's History

In Poems

1963- 2015

James R. Ellerston

imagine a better world (1914-2014)

one hundred years ago this year
"'twas the night before Christmas"
on the Western Front;
the guns on both sides became silent;
and lights appeared over the German lines;
voices joined in chorus,
sonorous sounds drifting across the no man's land
separating the sons of fathers and mothers—
the tired embattled men on both sides.

it began snowing,
obscuring a full moon;
"stille nacht" drifted on the night air;
food was lobbed into opposing trenches,
soldiers applauding each others singing;
Christ trees were erected on the German lines;
"don't shoot, we will send you some bier";
the opposing officers walked out, met, saluted;
the unofficial truth
was that they agreed not to fire on Christmas Day,
to meet and fraternize,
to play soccer between the wires;
the official truth was "a chance to bury the dead",
and read the 23rd psalm over the graves of both sides;
"He makes me lie down in green pastures";
but there was no green grass,
only frozen earth and snow beneath worn boots.

by commanders official orders the guns were not to be silenced again
until the eleventh hour of the eleventh day of the eleventh month,
after the four more years of carnage
which followed that one quiet day of Christmas peace in 1914.

James R. Ellerston
October 30, 2014

ultimatum 1939

yesterday September first in 1939
the pianist had stopped playing in a Polish radio station,
and a seventy-fifth anniversary is now observed;
Germany had attacked Poland,
and one half of Poland was taken over by the Russians;
(Russia attacked starting September 17th after the German crush;
the land Russia conquered has remained part of Russia since);
most of the world watched—
instead of appeasement and sanctions
the British gave an ultimatum
which ran out on the clock;
the king's speech bravely announced a state of war,
the British with their ally Poland would work together
to fight the Nazi German machine—
no appeasement this time,
no paper brought back from Munich,
no cease fires:
Britain fought on alone;
miracles with Spitfires over Dover
and small ships at Dunkirk;
(the war dragged on: Britain rationed food until 1954;)
a reluctant United States could not decide
to enter the game except with Lend-Lease;
(a capitalist Roosevelt understood the workings of credit)
first the phony war dragged on,
battles then raged on as German evil advanced;
no American boots on the ground for years,
only strikes from the air,
just like today,
until things developed into another World War.

James R. Ellerston
September 3 , 2014

Supermarine Spitfire (1940)

agile
acrobatic
repairable
inspiring to its young pilots,
a weapon for national survival
spinning white exhaust trails spiraling over Dover,
yet a burning cauldron for those shot-up;
the exceptional fighter plane that was Hitler's nemesis,
defending Britain when it stood alone against the Reich,
when so few with courage fought for so many;
stalling for time to build up its forces,
postponing the invasion of that noble island;
the hope of a nation those summer August and September days
in the Battle of Britain a soaring righteous bird,
a silver butterfly of imaginative engineering—
ultimately the machined design that saved civilization
at its most desperate moment.

James R. Ellerston
April 1, 2014

Dresden: Florence of the North to be No More (February 13-14, 1945)

Churchill decreed the picturesque German city of Dresden was to be no more;
It became a planned victim of Britain's war-time bombing's firestorm roar;
Over-night two days in February shells and phosphorus bombs rained from the sky,
Clustered together and pounded down on timbered houses so that even more would die.

In 2010 to count dead again there was a purposeful but not definitive commission,
but totaling numbers for vaporized corpses depends on a nation's political position;
War-torn refugees westward fleeing swelled the population caught in the traversed city,
Out in the open without shelter, the fighter-planes strafed weakened people without pity.

In 1996 a construction site turned up yet another smoldering body hidden decades lying;
The actual number of charred victims to bury, still disagreeing Allies arguing denying;
Some labeled this planned desecration of beauty and culture a crime against humanity;
Surely for the number killed and shrunken blackened it was an immeasurable atrocity.

A wind-driven blazing gaseous cauldron of centigrade sixteen-hundred degrees,
it sucked in silent screaming victims not strategic industrial combative factories;
Half-timbered houses densely packed blackened and turned to infernos of smoke,
Night saturation-bombing kindled burning victims before they terrified awoke.

For those who found shelter there was no gasped air for drawing dying calming breath,
Quick suffocation brought young children and old grandparents blue-skinned searing death.
Nearly eighty years later military tactical reasons are a subject of agonized international debate,
but history's unlearned errors of flaming horror, mutilation, murder yet remain Man's future fate.

James R. Ellerston
May 6, 2013

Dresden (Acrostic)

Destruction purposefully warfare done
Reduced to rubble and ash and cinders
Entire population enflamed in death
Sizzling phosphorous self-ignited pain
Devouring flames a storm man-made
Educated world mourns cultural loss
Nation at peace, united, rebuilt, strong.

James R. Ellerston
May 6, 2013

Still Digging For All The Truth

While there are stone and concrete memorials there,
archeologist still dig in the Polish forest clearing;
they shovel and sift through earth at *Sobibor,*
having done so since 2007.

Digging has recently revealed the brick foundations
of former gas chambers of evil—
yet another camp of death
added to the list by *Yad Vashem.*

A metal medallion in the shape of a Star of David,
a golden ring with inscription in Hebrew,
the stone circle of an open well for drawing water—
these artifacts speak of love and faith amidst death-filled reality.

Historians of truth are still at work, again, and still;
a rusted road sign outside the perimeter
pointed the trucks of human cargo to this dark location—
still directs the 'diggers' of truth to this place of horror.

James R. Ellerston
September 19, 2014

Siege of Leningrad: 882 or 900 Days Makes No Difference if You're Starving

The Nazis had encircled the area in their drive northeast to capture the city;
The destruction of so much czarist beauty which had been preserved was a pity;
The destruction of flour storage and burning caused decrees lowering the ration of bread;
As time went on horses were butchered while still alive in the streets and cut up for meat instead.

As time eked on all coal and firewood ran out, and the only warmth was from pages of books;
People took on a deathly cast, bent over, weak in movement, aged in looks;
Children became sick, to weak to get out of bed, after first being to weak to stand;
Eventually trucks made a road over ice ever thin when it was impossible to bring food on land.

Dark death like a dagger of hunger stalked the bombed-out streets of Leningrad;
What happened there in near nine hundred days makes the mourning world still sad;
There is a brave story how the beautiful city on the riverbanks held out so strong;
But adequate nourishment for the courageous populace did not hold out as long.

It was in the 1990's when they were still reburying the winter-frozen dead;
The million and a half the Soviet government could not get minimally fed;
At the time they buried the starved-dead bodies in big open common pits;
Now today a few are labeled in individual graves much more forever fit.

Hamburgers of human flesh were sold at sidewalk stands as horsemeat in the street;
Person's bodies were ground-up from necessity from their once-muscled shoulders to their feet;
People were cold and to survive at all took effort and mental effort and was a feat;
After the granaries were bombed there was nothing to eat but burned soil and dead body's meat.

There was always a long line and a question of what to have for one's next meal;
As the scythes of death marched through frozen snow and funeral bells missed their peal;
Tonight we'll eat from top to bottom the east dining-room wall, we can't afford to waste;
Many a morsel of a meal they choked down the aged wheat from layers of stale wallpaper paste.

There were the once mighty tanks the industrious factories' labor made,
Not used for city freedom, but for Stalin's plan of battle, the hungry people dearly paid;
In winter they hauled precious cargo and what they could on the treacherous Lagoda ice road;
Every auto, sled and truck on the nearly melting ice precariously carried its nourishing load.

There is a huge concrete monument in the city of St. Petersburg as it is called today;
Under it hundreds of children's bodies and beloved dead grandparents lay;
Because some people held out and struggled daily to evade what seemed an inevitable grave,
A contribution was made to the Nazis' defeat, their Soviet nation for Stalin to save.

James R. Ellerston
February 2, 2013

January 1946: The Code of Love

I think what kept Grandpa going at war
      when he'd fought to save this land,
Was something I've felt and seen each day
      and tried to understand.

Far up north in Wisconsin on a forest road or two,
Our lakeside house stands high on a hill
      beside a pine tree'd shore;
Preserved under glass above an upstairs bed
      I've seen this square of yellowed paper;
It's now just a little tattered and worn,
      And saved many long years from scrap,
I know it has to be an important note;
      It's never been thrown away.
I knew somehow it must be a clue
      hung high up on that wall;
Framed yellowed paper with faded ink--
      Spelling in hardly decipherable letters--
Sixteen chosen words of telegraph code
      that very plainly said:
Stop everything, Stop. I love you, Stop
      I'm coming home to you;
'Cause they could only send the code of love
      across the war-torn seas.

His ship rode over the ocean swells
      To the damp New Guinea sands;
He trudged dusty hills and endless mud
      On Philippine island roads.
He carried folded papers in his sweat-soaked shirts—
      Her letters near his heart;
He spent nights in rainy torrents
      near flooding watery banks.
They quickly bridged the rivers' shores
      with concentrated zeal;
The war moved ahead and men fought on--
      Needing bridges no matter what.
His outfit built pontoons and trusses for trucks
      And treads for advancing tanks;
They bridged high streams and valleys deep
      For the army to swiftly cross.
His daily letters sent homeward
      Were a pathway for loving thoughts;
'Cause they could only send the code of love
      across the war-torn seas.

All dreaded the plans for Japanese beachheads
        And roads to Tokyo if war dragged on;
Unneeded bridge plans stayed locked in his vault
        Because of the atomic bombs.
A few occupied months in defeated Japan
        delayed his slow journey homewar;
Slowly rebuilding the enemies war-ravaged land--
        To show the American sense of fair play—
Building bridges now from mind to mind,
        so Orientals would think democracy's way.

This man and this woman had written each day,
        Though from where in secrecy never to disclose:
Envelopes and letters he so carefully addressed--
        first and last name and something between;
He fit a new and different middle initial
        in their own made-up code games.
After mailing many letters home with little else to say,
        It finally spelled out a place:
For her to locate with some odd foreign words
        Upon the global space.
She would finally know his troops location,
        Unless they had already moved--
Once again shipped out and sent somewhere else--
        now unknown to her.
Many more letters he soon addressed
        And newly initialed her name;
'Cause they could only send the code of love
        across the war-torn seas.

From far across vast Pacific waves
        Their letters were filled with hope and love,
Written in the heart-felt code of youthful truth
        The censors would pass through;
Each day that message sent home from him
        Helped keep her waiting strong;
He knew each day she had written again
        She'd been faithful all along.
Finally he sent a message one day
        From a soldier who'd survived the long fight:
Passing along feelings with short dots and dashes
        in bold Western Union type.
His sixteen words were very strong
        Spelling out every soldier's dream:
(I)"Expect To Be Home Soon" (to you)

(So)"Don't Write Further" (here),
"I'll Contact You On Arrival" (home),
        "All My Love" (I send to you).
Grandpa signed his spelled out name,
        Written out in full;
'Cause they could only send the code of love
        across the war-torn seas.

When I was just a little boy
        I hoped to be so tall;
Soon upon a chair I'd stand,
        And my Grandma feared I'd fall.
Today I'm no longer a small little boy
        And stand full grown near six feet tall.
I sometimes remember and look when alone
        at Grandpa's yellowed and faded old note;
It's framed up high on the south bedroom wall
        In the house he built with his hands.
I remember what kept Grandpa strong overseas
        While he fought to save these lands:
Something I've felt and lived through the years--
        Really natural to understand.

In the up-north Wisconsin woods
        there is still brittle paper with faded ink,
        Hardly readable print at all;
Sixteen short words of typed telegraph code
        Spell out one truth of life:
Stop Everything, Stop. I love you, Stop.
        I'm coming home to you;
Nothing stronger is ever more important to say
        To one's child, parent, friend, or spouse.
Once it was just short cryptic phrases
        My Grandpa wired sixty years ago,
In urgent telegraphic brevity—
         sent homeward to one so true;
'Cause they could only send the code of love
        across the war-torn seas.

James Ellerston
May 21, 1995; February 11, 2003; October 24, 25, 29, 2007

Expect To Be Home Soon/ Don't Write Further/
I'll Contact You On Arrival/ All My Love
Walter E. Best
 January 1946
Lois Matteson and Walter E. Best were married February 2, 1946

World News

On the farm
in a house filled with my mother's volumes
my father never read a book—
but read three newspapers daily—
under increasingly brighter lamps
when his eyes did not keep-up
with the size of newsprint;
he loved the want-adds
and never discussed foreign affairs with me.

The nuclear shadow hung over our home
as the Omaha SAC planes created their sonic booms
over the innocence of our Iowa farm;
and my father bought sugar a hundred pounds at a time
and stored it hidden upstairs in a closet
while the bombs flew above us twenty-four hours daily
and Walter Cronkite talked on CBS
about missiles from Soviet ships in Cuba
and feed-sacks full of sand nudged the basement windows
in real fear.

there would be fall-out from world events
even this far from the Omaha airfield
when it was bombed.

James R. Ellerston
October 16, 2014

East German Border Guard Conrad Schumann

at 4 pm. on 15 August 1961 he was devoured by history;
it was two days after the regime began erecting the Wall in Berlin;
many people were standing around and so watched him jump,
and the shutter of a camera clicked open for an instant famous photograph,
of a man who later married, had a son, and worked at Audi.

coils of wire had been spread across the concrete which he guarded;
he had swapped out a loaded sub-machine for an empty lighter unloaded gun;
his nerves were at the breaking point, but in faith he took the leap,
to the western side of *Bernauer Straße* and a waiting car,
and a Cold War image was born.of black and white.

the picture of your lanky nineteen year old body soaring above coils of barbed-wire
blitzed across the world: you were condemned a homeland traitor (2100 guards fled with you)
because you did not want to "live enclosed" at home in the DDR;
a fit of desperation, or act of heroism, distinguishable only in each side's history;
the *Stasi* wanted their Cold War fleeing icon back, the photo retained its propaganda claims.

He eventually settled down to a life in a Bavarian village,
where this history man left no final farewell letter,
before he hanged himself from a wooded orchard tree;
this hero-traitor got nothing for his fame but a silver statue ,*Mauerspringer* (Wall Jumper)
now hanging from the side of a new building in the *straße* where he made his choice.

James R. Ellerston
March 16, 2014

In Remembrance of Peter Fechter

At age eighteen you 'only wanted freedom'
on 17 August 1962, when you hurled your body toward the divisive wires
running across the guarded 'no man's land'
between you and the insidious barbed and concrete fence.

You and a friend had decided you could straddle the wire,
and ran forward to escape to the West and your youthful hopes
amidst a hail of hostile bullets in your halting guarded path,
vicious fired at fleeing young fragile sprinting bodies.

Your friend made it over the wires, through to the helpful side,
but you lay bleeding-out before the bitter fence—
lay for fifty-nine minutes at the base of the new Berlin Wall,
while people on the Western side could only call-out for your aid.

Some threw bandages across the barricade as you posed wounded languishing,
becoming a Cold War martyr before the world's camera eyes;
after your demise famously carried away to a pronouncement of hospital death;
subject for a golden statue, you in the cradling arms of the man as idealized as you.

James R. Ellerston
March 14, 2014

"THE WALL"

Up looms a monument,
    No monument of gains.
A fence which holds in millions
    As if they were in chains.

It's built of blocks and barbwire,
    Set in mortar strong.
So it can work without tire
    To hold an Eastern throng.

Dividing families, friends, and foe,
    A sort of modern slavery.
A major cause of cries and woe
    A good example of tyranny.

An ugly sight, a shameful sight,
    Of gray and black and rust.
A monster, a huge thing
    Of giant towering height.

Persons risk their precious lives,
    To live on freedom's side.
To be shot down amidst the cries
    And fall to earth to die.

Now, if someday that wall comes down,
    'Twill be a blessing to recall.
And just another example of
    The power of freedom's mighty call.

                              May, 1964

"THE KANAUGA BRIDGE"

The bridge is in the river,
  it isn't any more,
That twisted mass of tortured steel,
  Not "strong and sturdy" as before,
Has wreaked its vengeance as it must,
  For its aged and creaking members,
Neglected as are some of us,
It too, soon fell to destruction;
  Choosing of its own free will,
To end the life of its construction
  And leave our hearts to pay the bill.

The bridge was jammed with travelers,
  Homeward bound they slowly went,
The best of them by ignorance
  and negligence were swiftly spent.
The Christmas shoppers many and merry,
  filled with thoughtful holiday cheer,
All hurried on, with the rest,
  Toward the ones that they held dear.
The traffic-- heavier than usual,
  No safety regulations given,
The cars and trucks crawled slowly forward,
  thicker than before,
The number-- near a hundred,
  All hurrying from shore to shore.

The steelwork jutted into the sky,
  It boasted iron will and strength,
It would have its way and they would die,
  On its graceful sloping suspension length.
It had forty years experience,
  It boasted of its size,
What the inspector looked for?
  It is difficult to surmise.
Two lanes wide, its length near two thousand feet,
  Above the river deep.
The bugs and ants crawling slowly home
  Were trampled under its thoughtless feet.
Eight specks of dust quick left the world;
  Many more were bruised.
The bridge had wreaked its vengeance,
  Its tortured mind was soothed.

December 12, 1967

"CAN WE COPE WITH FIRE?"

To protect the sacred governmental halls,
Eleven thousand troops guard Washington.
For the nation is in a burning war;
And every good soldier stands tall,
     and holds his deadly gun.

The pink cherry trees are blooming today,
But soft blossoms quickly fade and die.
Discouraged tourists have all gone home in fear;
For an ugly black cloud fills the once blue sky.

They say the nation is in an ugly light,
They tell me it is scorching smoke.
The capital city has been set on fire;
Brave fireman with hoses,
     the smoldering buildings soak.

The dark streets are empty and filled with fear,
The White House is surrounded by an iron fence,
A haggard President shows great concern;
His worried face is drawn and tense.

The noble city burned but once before,
When the British came from distant foreign shore.
The Capitol and White House went up in smoke;
But that was an act of actual war.

The people want equality
     and not this senseless burning,
Today we have a problem, not another civil war.
We need only to find a good talking point;
But only to reach it fast--
     or else, we'll be no more.

The black smoke is over Washington,
I know it is quickly burning.
The peace marches-- are they done with now?
Yes, turmoil and strife are violently stirring.

continued

Thick smoke is over Washington,
I've heard that "the country will soon be done."
With all the rest we idly stand,
        while watching the flames consume;
We know not how, or what to tell our questioning son.

But how can we cope with fire?
For the flames are burning hot,
We claim to be people-- but our hearts are cold;
More often than they are not.

So how can we sit and simply hope,
With only an idle half-hearted desire.
When we're suddenly forced, with it to cope;
Now that they're playing with fire.

April 7, 1968

First Lieutenant; red velvet, gold gilt (1969)

a Tuesday January 35, '68 or '69, or any day
sitting on a velvet pad,
of real red velvet and under gold gilt,
beneath the whiteness of a frosted roof,
with yellow sunlight streaming in
through many crystal panes
set in their sham colonial frames
in walls of brick and plaster.
where crystal lights hang
from white suspended
above red carpet thick,
in a building called a church;
a place of purity
where an organ plays, and choirs sing,
and people pray to God.
today people come uncomfortable
and sitting stare: to pay respects;
respects for the dead and dying;
to the First Lieutenant, red velvet, gold gilt.

the program read,
the program for the spectacle—
that a man had given his life
as a Lieutenant in the Army,
had died in hostile action
in a swamp (desert) across the sea—
and is now but a flag draped casket,
in a world of deadly wrong.
he was born like any boy,
graduated from the city's high school,
even attended college, or tried,
enlisted in the service 19—
etc. etc. etc. … until his death;
his life now nothing—but a half-masted flag,
a few trophies of the games of war and life—
a First Lieutenant, red velvet, gold gilt.

what of one's life?
where are his loves and hopes,
the childish thoughts of a summer's day,
when all that is left are the medals of bronze:
the trophies of the games of war and life,
and a few kind mournful words?
when the sham of gold gilded lights
shimmer cheaply on velvet and glass
amid the echoing words of a promise,
the promise of God above looking down,
Who sends life to people and then takes it back;
a God above seeing all—
the flag draped coffin, a dead soldier—
the First Lieutenant, red velvet, gold gilt.

choirs of praising voices sour shout
and shriek in hope and fear:
we have a rock,
though all hearts of men are set against us,
and through all the weapons of war—
we have hope—they sing.
yet on the blackened side of earth
the deadly bullets fly
under a choking roof of smoke;
the blinding light of glaring flares
fire the blued-steel guns of pain;
there also a gasping breath for life--
as aching people pray to God in hell,
and scream in pain for his salvation—
with hopes for fleeting death.

take any January 35th,
the people sitting chanting loud,
and having hope –for nothing here, but there—
and with the bloody colors of stained gauze flags,
the manufacturing of coffins continues
under the choking roof of smoke;
they await their destined duty--
the first lieutenants— until we add red velvet,   James R. Ellerston
and must add our own guilt.   Jan. 1969, May 5 2008

American History Class 1969

I October
I'm sitting in history class
waiting for the teacher;
George Washington died a long time ago;
the Vietnam Moratorium is next Wednesday;
the Mu Gamma Pi pledge banquet
is more consequential
than the Jeffersonian ideals.
the professor arrives;
rumors start;
anyway back to George Washington
--it's just about time--
it ended years ago.

II. November
wonder why the chatter stopped?
American History, George Washington;
he stalks in staring
at the orange and purple stage lights;
the test is not yet corrected;
the prevailing set of ideas changed
(our foreign entanglements
through the remainder of the century)
for those that flunked:
became pre-occupied
with domestic problems.
and the whole problem of slavery,
wars--
advancing into new territories,
moving on through time;
in the Revolutionary Era:
just ticking off some of these things,
waiting for the bell.

III. December
the sun blocked out
by night's dark clouds;
we hit each other's hearts
with blocks of ice;
as we all grew older.
knowing that somewhere,
in another world
was love;
while on the dormitory desk
George Washington   James R. Ellerston
lay in aging pain.   December 16, 1969

October 1, 1969:
The Draft Lottery

I'm number 305, who's that?
Come back number 23;
Come back number 18;
Like the highway to doomsday
you go forth from this place,
toward the invisible horizon;
Go in Peace.

Why is it
All the people I've really cared about
keep leaving?
Except me.

December 1969
James R. Ellerston

II. Encore (1969)

The college sun shone through the glass windows
Under the concrete dome
     smelling of French fries and hamburgers;
The draft lottery had been a week ago;
Number 2, He is leaving for the Army
     (and Vietnam) tomorrow;
He says "Why did you play that song…
     Are you trying to make me cry?"
And I felt embarrassed by the feelings
     my quarter caused;
But the juke box kept on playing:
"I'll be there, I'll be there, I'll be there."
Forty years later sitting in the darkened auditorium,
Remembering, I sing along and shudder at the reprise.
All those young singers with no number
     attached to their birthdays
Get to dance their youth and make music not war.

April 25, 2008

#305 James Ellerston

I Saw a Dog Killed in the Street Today
(Confronting Death)

I saw a dog killed in the street today;
I stood and stared.
but little did it matter—
traffic flowed on as usual
and you went on your way.

I stood transfixed and watched
as the warm life spilled out
onto the pavement stone;
the scarlet mixed with slush
and the very first snow of winter.

I stood and stared there
as my heart spilled out—
onto the jungle floor of Vietnam;
into a street of Pakistani refugees;
into war and hate and disrespect
and all the other "Whys?"

A man came along and saddened looked;
his thick brown shoes and heavy gloves
stopped for the warm life
spilled out onto pavement stones;
Guessed he'd better do something—
(put him out of his misery).

We three looked together
into the soft brown eyes
yet warm with master's trust
and filled with puppy's love;
the scarlet mixed with the slush—
one life, a grain of dust;
we were with death on the pavement stone,
in the jungle grasses of Vietnam.

I saw a dog killed in the street today;
I stood and stared;
death did not matter.
Traffic flowed on as usual;
the world went on its way.

December 16, 1970   James R. Ellerston

The Shadow

I suppose I shall always be haunted
by the fear
that someday someone will say to me,
"Daddy, what did you do about the war?"
And I shall have to reply,
"I went to work as usual."

April 1972
James R. Ellerston

Challenger Disaster

I.

I have a dream hidden deep down
in a part of me I don't visit very often;
I hold a dream inside tucked somewhere
in the back of my internal closet.

II.

I have a memory in an old cardboard box (1960)
covered with flowing photos of adventure;
Held together with tape
is that small rocket model,
all authentic in detail
wrapped in old Weekly Readers,
and newspaper headlines held together
with snowy visions of black and white television
in the school cafeterias of innocence.

III.

I have a memory of that day at home in 1963;
Wrapped in a blanket against the November chills,
on a day home from junior high school,
I watched the long parade
And saw the child salute;
The slow horse drawn wheels rolled on the street;
The loss was beat into my mind
with the cadence of the drums;
We are a generation that remembers
where we were that day and heard the news.

IV.

I have a memory of a summer day in 1969;
I have a memory of a fishing trip to a Minnesota lake,
And of a small eleven-inch black and white screen;
This was the kind of little T.V. that had a traveling case
and fit in car trunks next to Dad's duffel
and mother's overstuffed overnight bags;
The black and white image was clear in the summer air;
There was a man in a light colored suit on light ground;
He made footprints as he bobbed with the joy of youth
and radioed back "one giant step for all mankind";
My father mumbled something about all the good
that much money could have done on earth;
While I watched the moon through the picture window;

It was a full moon
and was reflected on the stillness of the lake
as mosquitoes swarmed against the screens
and waves lapped the shore;
I loved my country and all it stood for—
that flag standing in the lunar dust;
I looked many times from the water to the sky
to the flickering screen—
all the time thinking "Man is there."

V.

As an adult (1983) I found myself carrying the toddler
in the backpack past the German V2's,
past the Wright brothers' plane—
overwhelmed with joy as I raced
past the Smithsonian exhibitions;
Yes, it's all here;
My fingers traced the screws holding
the plexi-glass protection over the Apollo capsule;
The capsule was sheathed in plastic,
protected from being worn way
by the hands and fingers
of people like me touching the real thing.
The twenty minute wait dragged slowly,
but finally I was inside skylab;
The line pushed on;
There were so many controls in there;
I wondered what it felt like with the hatch closed—
in space;
The crowd pushed on;
The sunlight and click of the camera
and the reassurance of the familiar flashbulb image
marked my crossing of the stellar path;
We hadn't allowed enough time to see it all.

VI.

The new technology has brought color pictures
and the television now shows the space shuttle;
Now a teacher I crowd with students into the library
to see the first shuttle land;
The calm voice of the news announcer narrates
the beautiful glide holding all our hopes
in the air of silence
at the perfect roll across the white sand;
The sunshine and grace of the landing are the finale
after days of suspenseful newscasting.

VII.

Strange photos have crowded my eyes;
The last few days have shown me strange worlds
in a planet they don't pronounce the same
as my sixth grade science teacher did
while we pasted in the pictures cut and trimmed
from the Sunday paper into our spiral notebooks;
We have seen the black and white photos
again on the screen—the unexpected moons,
the hidden valleys of deep canyons,
and high mountains,
through the rings of debris;
The excitement was all back again:
Look at those pictures
and the teacher going into space.

VIII.

On January 28, 1986 my jaded indifference
is shocked back into perspective
as my students file in
to tell me the latest radio reports;
Class activities are suspended
as the static of the radio conveys no hope;
I rush home to a three year old daughter
who says, "Did you see the ---plosion?"
I am subjected and barraged
with countless video replays
of the spreading orange light,
the white smoke,
the President's message,
the shocked faces;
Can it ever be the same again?

IX.

I hold a dream of space travel;
I want to keep it;
I want it to go on;
It formed my generation in our youth;
It is in the back of our minds
as a belief in what man can do.

January 28, 1986
James R. Ellerston

Twenty-Eight Years

It was a celebration with the world
with someone to somehow share—

I.

November 9, 1989
The quick trip to the shopping mall;
flip on the radio;
The news bulletin at 4:00 p.m.
kept me in the car for ten minutes;
I am choked with joy, and eyes are moist.

In the store business went on as usual—
Cash or Charge?

I hurried home to watch the news;
My wife watched and said she didn't remember—
that she had been in grade school
(four years younger is the difference in age
between eleven and seven).

II.

August, 1961
The Sunday Des Moines Register came;
The young boy grabbed the Picture Magazine;
On the front was that unforgettable photo,
of he young acrobat of a soldier
leaping across the coiled wire at his feet—
with that look of determination in his eye;
And later story after story to read
in the big weekly magazines long gone:
Life, Look, and Post.

III.

8th grade: 1964
To satisfy an English assignment
the adolescent boy cut pictures
from the three great journals of the human soul,
and put them in a booklet
with the carefully changed wordings
that schoolchildren always use when writing term papers
(all outlines and note cards aside);
In the front after the required ten point outline
that all English teachers require—
was something different
(the reason all English teachers teach English);
There was a handwritten poem;
It was a strange thing for a fourteen year old farm boy
to feel compelled to include.

IV.

1964-1989
For twenty-five years so careless time spent;
in dresser drawers and cardboard boxed,
or on bookshelves filled with college texts,
and over-stuffed file-drawers of income-tax records;
The glue gradually came of the back of the pictures;
When they dropped off the cover
a sentimental hand touched them carefully
and tucked them into bed inside;
This historical record must be saved to be shared;
It became part of the collection of boxes
that made a three bedroom ranch house
seem small for a family of four.

V

June 12, 1987.
Ronald Reagan, the movie star rancher turned U.S. President
stands in front of Brandenburg Gate;
Protected from possible snipers from East Berlin
by sheets of bullet proof glass he loudly shouts,
"Mr. Gorbachev, open this gate.
Mr. Gorbachev, tear down this wall;"
 the echo sounds across history

VI.

November 9, 1989
The grown man rummaged through the stacks
of dusty cardboard boxes in the basement,
amidst the children's broken toys
and leftovers of past successes;
At last the small hand bound booklet was found.
Inside were the sheets of three-holed notebook paper,
Now no less readable for the dust and mildew;
The news and pictures on the television were amazing;
they were actually on top of it;
One man had a pick-ax;
they were passing it around;
The Iron Curtain was coming down.
At least in Berlin
they were actually on top of it;
Many men had shovels and pipes
and hammered it to the ground.

November 10, 1989
Revised October 3, 2008
James R. Ellerston

Freedom's Child

I am freedom's child in the arms of a mother;
The glimmer of a candle in Wenceslas Square shines in my eyes;
I am freedom's child on my father's shoulders
being carried forward by the current of reunification,
through the Brandenburg Gate across the Wall that is no more;
I sing a song of peace and brotherhood.

I am freedom's child still clutched in anguish,
in the grips of my mother's hopes for me;
My childish face is now at peace,
spattered with the mud of a Romanian mass grave,
still in my mother's arms;
I am but a statistic of historical brutality.

I am freedom's child wearing the uniform of my country proudly;
I am returning in the arms of a military transport plane
swaddled in the flag of the country I served;
The heat of the Panama tropics under the embalmer's die
still shows on my sun tanned youthful face;
I followed orders and distant deployment
Because of a belief in democracy as a solution.

I am freedom's child huddled over a steam vent
or sleeping in a shelter;
I go to bed tonight in fear;
Will I eat tomorrow or be beaten again?
Will I be jolted from the middle-class playground
of life and mid-career that I have known?
Will I enter into the impoverished workhouse
of the unemployed, the downsized,
the stagnation of the redundant worker
in a slowed economic financial crisis;
I am freedom's child just as much
now that I am a single divorced parent
and the bank has foreclosed my mortgage.

I am the child of the freedom of choice;
God finds me wrapped in a cocoon of suffocating plastic
and tossed into the dumpster with the sterile refuse
from a hospital or unplanned family clinic;
Will I serve no earthly embryonic purpose
or participate in no harvest of stem cells?
No candle of martyrdom ever gleamed in my eye;
No song of liberty ever left my lungs;
I did not chant with the thousands
at the feet of "Good King Wenceslas" repeatedly
"Let me live my own life."
The tyrants fell and live they could.

                                    January 6, 1990
                                    James R. Ellerston

Homecoming

Amid the gray piles of body bags
the bands play proudly;
And under red, white and blue skies
75,000 troops have already been returned home:
The flags once draped then folded--
now turned plastic wave in the hands of little school-children.
This stifling gush of patriotism
bursts forth from the stench of war,
suppressing the news broadcasts,
drowning out ten thousands engines of war,
anguishing our still-knotted stomachs:
Today's paper- there were three more non-combat deaths reported,
bringing the score
(to nearly include him)
almost equal the combat total
of this year's war.

For me the war is not over
until my boy comes home--
he crosses the sunlit space between us;
he has survived his time and gone the distance:
until the gravel on the drive crunches beneath
the high-topped boot of his stride,
our eyes meeting with a thousand-question gaze;
until the one answer in locked embrace,
our lives closer than they will ever be again--
two chins driven deep into opposing shoulders;
until his unlocked fears form rivers down my shirt,
and my brine of joy mingles with the salt pools on his back.
His vision is toward his future now freed;
mine looks back to the brief time we shared.

Fill for me the summer air with smells:
of teen-age mechanic's shade-tree grease,
the cherished leather of a new baseball glove,
and the familiar odor of Ivory soap
mixed with clouds of baby powder
wafting cumulus upon the breeze.
Over it all the faint tinkle of a music box
can be heard playing from a distant nursery window
now suddenly opened.
The pulsing beat of a rock band
cascades from the pickup as he waves from his seat
and is finally home.

April 8, 1991
James R. Ellerston

WHEN THE ONLY RIGHT ANSWER WAS FLOWERS IN A SPRING THAW

I.

Their game had passed to a different court;
The home court advantage had been worn down;
There's a crying need for televising to a different game plan
after trying to write down the loss at Dunblane School;
Grief presses on our economics driven electronic media hearts
and searches for coverage of the yellow-taped bleeding bullet
scene sprayed in pain before the camera's eye tear-fogs up;
There is no flotilla of Dunkirk miracle-boats this time
to bring the kindergarten youngsters back across the channel
between life and the deep river crossed to the shores of death.

II.

The muffled drums sound forth across Scotland;
The pipes drone and chant,
sob and wail,
calling across the hills and down the lanes of Britain,
the weeping notes of parenthood to all the world;
This is a lament swelling forth in heaving waves
across throbbing seas
of emotion filled heavy chests
encased in oceans of tear;
there is a voice singing from choked throats
a song of lost innocence,
singing across even barriers of different tongues
and guarded borders,
a universal dirge on a single spinning globe
of grieving common humanity—
and a callous world is brought nauseated to its sinking knees;
The crippling pain of unreality shocks spasmodic nerves
by the shooting of a teacher and a classroom of children
and defiles daily routines of black and white order;
Life is stained with dead bloodied children;
The cozy morning newsprint bleeds red
as many began their slumbering day in bed
and thumbed through their financial-woven worlds
constructed between the safety of paper sheets
and corporate public images;
They now dozed in dawning horror
to the broadcasters clock-radio world of energy.

III.

The cold-hearted senselessness crackled gray
across the telephone lines and instantaneous data transmissions;
The guilt of satellite-invasion and microwave-intrusion
surgically knifed open the gaping pain of a peaceful town
in a way which sickened even the least-ethical stomachs
of newsroom career-lifers in their mad press
on the most private moments of families;
We would have brashly thrust our microphones
before the mouth of the Father
even after the last sponges of vinegar
had long been delivered to the hand-bleeding Son;
Only eternal love penetrated the shrouds of darkness
covering the side-pierced earth trembling in pain.
The veil of decency was not parted.

IV.

World citizens responded with notes and teddy-bears;
Tear-it-down money promises a new school building and memorials;
Pompous dignitaries are touched momentarily genuine,
staggering beneath the weight of real leadership required
simply to carry-on and muddle-through another day;
March winds sneak around corners of school buildings
blowing unhindered through unoccupied sunlit spaces
where before the wee-ones had gathered in playful glee;
Soft tear drops torrent from tissue-draped weeping skies
erasing the last of winter's embracing frosty blankets
shockingly drawn thoughtless back rude in careless haste
exposing the fourteen tiny bed of deeply spaded earth;
These await new floral spring linen replacements
after the grieving florists' proper cellophane-wrapped bouquets
lie exposed from melting snows.

V.

Ward off the windy drafts and provide renewing body-clothes
of greenest grass and perfumed flowers;
Wait for the headstones atop now arrested childhood
to roll back like the seas of Moses
parting until the chariots passed;
Let the game resume after all this time-out in life's script;
The years of game-time should continue for these children
without a single foul morbid terminating act;
The entire cast of the play was put out too soon--
before the happy ending we all desire for our children
(as we cope with the reality of our own mortality).

VI.

A child sized concrete angel lies broken at the waist
knocked over by youthful thoughtless vandals;
It crudely stares in stone vision paralyzed
upward toward the heavens;
Desperation chokes out an anguished question of reason;
Absent little footprints in the greening lawns
in each family yard
do not stare back at fathers' tending nurturing hands,
now weeding and watering memories and visions
of imaginary games of ball and tag;
Mothers struggle through once ordinary family rituals;
Mothers unable again to tuck a breathing little loved-one
in between the white-sheet plains of cotton flannel
and the billowy comforter-mountains of warming-snuggle
that now map out the empty beds of tear-drowned rivers of grief;
Dream-haunted aging hands splash between dishwater banks
on the darkened down-river drift of survival and search
for some rational reason within the limits of grief filled years.

VII.

The centuries-older stones of Scotland's churches
are swathed in coiled razor-wire;
Such barbed protection keeps lead-flashed roofs
and stained seamed window glass from harms way;
It prevents total social transformation into insane violence;
Clasped majority-hands pray with earnest unfamiliarity
to a once-minority God newly accessible
in current desperation as a nation begs for hope
from its historic past to provide a future vision;

The world assembles in spirit beneath the slate roofs
of a nation baptized by the senseless slaughter
of pastoral innocence gone somehow wrong,
despite the nurturing in small-town values;
Dreams once flowering
Were mowed down in a swath
across the kindergarten of life;
No blood on Hebrew lintel-posts
saved their young from the bullet-strewn plague.

VIII.

These broken angels are now cast in death
Because life's stone was chiseled out
and shattered by one man's raging anger;
We have been humbled in defining limits
of decency in time of human loss
and can cause a world press
of curiosity to step back in respect;
I question my right
to know anything at all
about parents' private pain and loss,
and the lessons to be learned through studying
the tough course on life and love
taught in the school at Dunblane;
After the brutal massacre
the only right answer in Dunblane
was flowers in a spring thaw.

April 3, 1996
James R. Ellerston

with amazing grace they stood

until they fell one dark September 11, 2001
the Twin Towers graced the Manhattan skyline,
the New York skyline, the nation's skyline,
a fixture of the lead-in to every apartment sit-com,
recognizable on every television set in America.

an amazing feat of engineering—
the utilization of a daring challenge to the typical skeletons
of tall buildings climbing skyward toward the heavens;
it wasn't internal frameworks of beams supporting the 110 floors
but exterior walls meant to stand as long as the Jerusalem Temple.

the Staten Island ferry heaved across the harbor to the city
under my uncontrollable whooshing college-age stomach,
as we crossed between the populous shores
of suburban New Jersey and the beaches of Staten Island
the ship rising and falling in the tidal swells

we moved toward the island of the American dreamers,
dwarfed in 1970 by cranes and twin orange skeletons
reaching beyond the ceiling of previous imaginative engineering;
advancing walls rising upward toward the limits of support—
after the fires a structural system hastily outlawed in building codes.

after the *jihad* plane crashes the architect had his negative thoughts—
that he would never be allowed to build again;
webs of structural floor steel had sagged and failed
as flames engulfed their tensile strength and poor fire retardants;
drywall fought to protect evacuation stairs in a cauldron of fire.

crushing dust and screaming people filled America's television sets,
the President spoke, jets were scrambled,
the Pentagon became another terrorized deadly target;
brave souls in a plane over Pennsylvania prevented another attack,
ending brave lives in a field of debris forever memorialized.

the next Sunday, a grieving September 16th
church choirs across the nation sang to numb congregations,
immersed in fervent prayers for the nation,
for strength, condolence, forgiveness and flag.
our choir sang that with God's grace we would be eternally there.

Our own choir sang that our lives as a strong nation
would shine out to the world the light of their faith in love.
It is in the forgiveness and understanding of our Islamist brothers
that has shown the real glowing healing of America's hearts;
the goal to shine in God's sun for one thousand years.

I think of that Sunday September 16th when we sang out our words,
powerful music that moved some to tears, choked others up;
my throat tightens each time we sing of the shining sun—
today shining down on memorial pools and a new diamond spire,
again challenging those who would throw stones against us.

we sing this each time surrounded by ripples of liquid sound,
waves of harmonies; with a *rubato* for a quiet time in prayer—
a robust spirit of melodic survival reminds us
that there were repeated patterns in the steel facade
and in the musical mind of a talented Mark Hayes.

our planet Earth continues rotating with its populous seas of culture
and islands of progressive love while others endure pain and hatred--
but only half of it is ever in the warmth of the sun
for the Christian world it is the Son of God
carrying it through cold-hearted times.

James R. Ellerston
March 4, 2014

Crew of Columbia: Gems of the Ocean of Space

On ancient scholars' wings of daydreams and drifting thought
      wise men of old longed to soar in aerial flight,
To rise somehow above cursed earth's accusing scorching fight;
Yes, lift our fitful dreams from hunger and seething scornful daily blight,
      and soar with timely scheduled will,
      with glaring rockets' thundering might;
To float free: not with feebly weighted skin-clothed bodies,
      but dressed in silver shields through universal star-filled night;
Science strove with genius from endless imagination for all mankind,
      leaving gravity-bound mathematicians pondering below
          numerous mental burdens of computerized numbers
          exact to the million but never slight;
Skilled technicians built unending newly crafted engine designs
      while previous problems were scoffed at and gladly shouldered light.

Isolated pilots spun and daily flew in constant risk of deadly harm,
      countlessly orbiting miles above anxious families' loving prayerful sight;
Crews birdlike sailed dependent on others and so certain to voyage alive,
      because of masterful team-mates assigned the difficult work below:
Hundreds in watchful televised toil created an umbilical electronic control
      with wave-formed beams to fly a craft above
          as a heaven-borne stringless gleaming kite;
Her unguarded gliding gone misshapen caught on jagged nerves' alarm,
      at once unprecedented chaos and sudden tragic belated plight
          to quickly set the mission now awry
          once again calm and somehow right;
A sky team triumphant was returning home happy and proud
      with all tasks achieved and skillfully done with challenges set aright,
They would have been full lifetime friends,
      bonded by experience and bound tight.

Among us below are those who would feebly and weakly dare in fright,
      and can never somehow do it quite;
We are born to watch from afar the larger inspired forging footprints wight
      of the few real giants who have the rightmost leading strength;
We wishfully admire and praise their "stuff",
      but stand alone in inept regret's delight.
True heroes are chosen by unsurpassed and unforeseen courage:
      Those valiant who rise through written history's path unplanned now bright,
          through accident of nature, time, and site,
          are forever engraved in eyes of children's vision at such ultimate height.
The crew of 'Columbia" commenced their untimely moment's path to alight,
      towards God's strong wisdom of gentle forgiveness without spite;
Through a single relentless instant entered by blinding flash and bitter bite,
Souls at rest have now attained salvation's final journey into the eternal white .

              James Ellerston   February 1, 2003

wight--adj. Brit. Dial. 1. strong and brave, esp. in war 2. active, nimble
aright-- adv. rightly, correctly, properly
alight--v.i. 1. to dismount from a horse, descend from a vehicle etc. 2. to settle or stay after descending
      3. to encounter or notice something accidentally
tight-- adv. 19. in a tight manner; closely; firmly; securely; tensely 20. soundly or deeply

Death of An Architect (Sydney Opera House)

The lights were dimmed in sorrow's mourning;
The great curves were darkened against
the night-time evening harbor breeze;
One brief hour blackened after dusk
to mark the passing of the great designer
of white-tiled fabric thrust windward
against the seaward blast;
These sails are held in concrete shape forever
against the pull of gravity,
against the limitations of mathematical computations;
A song-full voice sings forth an aria of cortege;
A chorus of persons the world over stops in contemplation
of the pictures in their morning newspaper—
Recognizing this symbol of Australia
that rose upward after years of controversy
and courageous builders' efforts;
Now as recognizable as the great pyramids of Egypt
this icon constructed in Sydney
is a monument for all mankind.
As the earth's spin rotated eastward toward the sun
we marked the passing yesterday of Joern Utzon,
Danish innovator, architect, and genius,
who with a few ink-strokes
drawn on a restaurant paper napkin
soared all our minds above the salted harbor of our passage,
winged all our toiling wave-tossed souls toward greater good.

There are no Wright horizontal lines here,
or rectangles in cantilevered balance;
There are only arcs curving compromised skyward
to fit the calculations of circular geometry,
compression loads and stresses;
Glass windows like eyelids are forever blinked open
nightly staring at the harbor
brilliantly illuminating man's art,
his successes and failures;
The operatic acts of man simply play out on God's stage
until the scenery concept is earthbound no longer—
The orchestrations once before tied to practical concerns
of underground parking-garages and acoustics,
and planted in family and home,
rooted in the basics of food, clothing, and energy,
are somehow by some creative compositions
floated yet heavenward above man's carbon footprint;
These buildings once built inspire us to our finest ideals.
Joern Utzon, son of Denmark, son of Australia,
is also son of the world;
His final curtain has come down;
His music and poetry of innovation live forward;
Our minds yet sing his soaring melody
in our own life theater,
acting on our daily stage,
following the sketch of His pen.   December 1, 2008
                                                    James R. Ellerston

Mahler Symphonique in 5:00 a.m. Psychology:
Orwellian Doublespeak August 6- August 21, 2008

I.

The commentator claims he knows the truth:
the Georgian war is the most significant event
since the fall of communism.
I see images of Russian tanks
parked peacefully on the highways of Georgia;
The oil of the Caucasus has been under contention
since Hitler's ill-fated drive on Stalingrad.
Yet I do not see any young "Hungarians" in the TV images
throwing rocks at the Russian tanks;
I do not see a young Chinese boy standing alone
in the Tiananmen Square in the middle of Gori--
stopping a tank by sheer guts and will power.

Instead I see the posturing of diplomats—
Sarkozy, the French President, has just returned from Munich,
giving the Russians the green light
to occupy the Sudetenland.
Excuse me, it is not 1938 but 2008 (South Ossetia).
Sarkozi steps off the plane in France
holding aloft a paper just the same.

The larger issue is when will the next war be in the Crimea:
We will fight in 2018 instead of 1848
over the approaches to the harbor at Sevastopol,
on the Black Sea.
The Russian Navy will fight for control of "their sea"
now as then.
And another incident in the Gulf of Tonkin will
embroil us in a new Vietnam.
Will Florence Nightingale please sweep down
with Humanitarian aid to prevent the ethnic cleansing
that has come to characterize the battlefield germ fighting
of all twenty-first century wars.

The anti-Semite Russians claim there was a "pogrom"
against the Ossetians, the ethnic Russians, and people of Abkhazia;
They deserve the chance to be free and join the greater Russian Reich.
Diplomats rush about on C-span
and ambassadors are interviewed,
but commentators tell us what they said,
as if we aren't smart enough to listen for ourselves.
Only once do they tell us
that there was not freedom of the press in Georgia:
their democracy is not our democracy.
We are told to feel more compassion for them
over a blown-up railroad bridge,
(their "Golden-Spike" between east and west Georgia),
then over the briefly shown images
of a smashed up television station that belonged to American TV.
The goose-stepping storm troopers of president Saakashvili
no longer are the SA smashing old-fashioned printing presses.
They now smash television cameras and satellite networking;
Broadcast media wars are now fought
with emotion laden words like democracy and freedom.

                              II
I wait again in an America of isolation.
Condoleeza flies the globe;
We will send humanitarian aid—
Once again we acknowledge that the powerful
has placed less fortunate people in camps.
Refugees have swarmed the woods and mountains—
but we never see them in our living rooms.
I never see a young "Hungarian" throwing rocks
and turning the smiling faces riding the Russian tanks
into torched and scarred bodies with Molotov cocktails.
Where is the "freedom-loving" populace?
Perhaps they are a figment of our willful imagination.

The Domino Theory is raised again:
After Georgia next Ukraine, Poland, the Czech Republic.
(It is ironic that the old men are still saying "Czechoslovakia").
But Condoleeza rushes in to tell the world
that we will place defensive missiles in "Cuba",
and they will be no secret this time.
The United States will stand by its allies this time.
But the fat men have sat around the table before—
dividing the world into spheres of influence.
Despite all promises to the contrary,
we have not stood by Poland ever,
least of all in 1945.

The larger question is still nuclear containment.
The government of Pakistan will have a new president;
The pro-US president has been forced to resign.
We are concerned when democracy takes a detour.
Iran and North Korea must not get the bomb. Alas!
We worked harder to assure the world
that Hitler wouldn't get the bomb
than we have worked in North Korea:
We leaked away Hitler's heavy water
and built a thousand centrifuges ourselves.
Canada is the leading manufacturer of heavy water today,
but we support NAFTA so we believe in the free market economy.
We promise the North Koreans "light water" reactors
to quit uranium enrichment in the heavy water reactors.
We never insist that those who sold them heavy water
be punished.
What industrialized country manufactured
the precision Iranian centrifuges?

Angela Merkel parades the power
of modern Germany before the world:
but she is the victim of a cold winter
and a long oil and gas pipeline stretching east.
There will be no convoys
to win the Battle of the Atlantic this second time.
The oil for Britain
does not come from the US any longer.
Germany will be cold without Russian gas,
and no well-heeled west German
will be happy to share his airlifted bag of coal
to defend (1948) 2008 Berlin
along with the unfortunates who joined Germany
from the eastern part of the country in unification.

So where does this leave us now?
The US President is on vacation at a Texas ranch
while the Russian troops roll across an international border.
He speaks to aged veterans at the VFW in Florida
while Russians dig in to checkpoint positions inside Georgia;
The Russian invasion is a reality
and we will "have peace in our time". Alas!
The ghosts of the czars march:
The greater Russian Reich will be reconstructed.

I am again eleven years old.
War planes in formation fly in the SAC scramble
booming sonically in the air above an Iowa farm;
The fear of nuclear war is present and streaking harsh
in white streams across the sunlit sky.
Black and white television images
display in shades of gray the wisdom of blockade
and a show of force by Navy ships..
Our young President looks suddenly older, wiser, and aged.

My family stockpiles sugar and potatoes,
and piles of bizarre canned goods which later turn to rust.
Basement windows are sandbagged,
with sacks that once held only the hope of a profit on hogs.
We draw a picture of our house plan
and send it in to Civil Defense.
We are told "stay in your basement
and cover the kitchen floor above it with books".
We believe that stacks of pieces of paper will save us.
At the high school I take Geiger counter training.
We volunteered and signed a paper each session
with the amount of radiation we were exposed to.
There is a shortage of young manpower on the farms;
Many young men go first to Germany and then on to Vietnam.
Many never return, and those that do are not the same.

I win the most important lottery of my life with number 305
and am excluded from the draft by virtue of my birthday.
I do not waste my life with grass and drugs,
and age through university, raising a family, and retirement.
I am now on vacation
when the television (which will soon go digital)
brings the same news of conflict.
But this time the search is for the truth,
and in late middle-age I am a cynic.
The young man whose father went to Harvard before him
portrays himself as one of us;
Or I can choose the older man--
perhaps he is wiser.
A POW-MIA flag flies above the beach outside my window:
The older man tells the story
of how he chose to free another man first—
before he would allow himself to be freed.
His audience fights back tears.

VII

My body swims through contented warmth;
my feet walk on even sand.
The atmosphere swirls around me;
the sky is blue;
the wind blows softly.
Our aged bodies plow determined forward through the surf,
parting the lake with youthful energy and enthusiasm.
She says "this must be what heaven is like".
And I remember her saying it
and write it down like truth and gospel.

VIII

I stockpile bottled water again.
This is no Katrina or Midwest flood:
but only that once again
the federal government has failed to respond properly.
I wait for the victor to withdraw—
There is nothing within civilized reason we can do.
I wait for an image
of a young "Hungarian" throwing a rock at a tank.
Where is the populace
that should be showering the tanks with Molotovs?
At the least where are the roadside bombs
(which have killed and maimed so many Americans so successfully)?
I see images of blind-folded prisoners riding on tanks
while the Russian soldiers smile at the TV crews;
I see images of the old and infirm
slowly walking in hopeless isolation.

IX

The US puppet government in Georgia has fallen? Alas no!
US anti-missile missiles have been removed
from Poland and the Czech Republic.
Obligations to Poland have once again been negotiated away:
And she will cede the eastern third of her nation to Russia—
After all Finland deserved this in the Winter War
for defending herself in 1939 on skis.

X

The Russians celebrate drinking Vodka.
Americans have a new fad of drinking bottled water.
The "shining city on the hill" is tarnished—
unable to fight
more than a few desert and mountain skirmishes at a time.
Afghanistan was freed from British rule 89 years ago
and Russian rule one and a half decades ago.
Afghanistan was freed from American rule next week?
The challenge is imminent.

XI

New York City Building Code Revision:
Never again will towering skyscrapers be built
with the acknowledged defects in structural engineering
which could fail due to inadequate fire-preventative insulation
on steel trusses.
Media blamed the Taliban, not architectural error.

XII

I have seen one Chinese boy stop a tank in a city square.
I have not seen a Georgian Molotov stop a single tank
and horribly burn its victorious drivers
like the poor RAF pilots who were so horribly burned
in the great battle "when so many, owed so much, to so few".
Give me someone today who can smoke a cigar
in the face of wrong.

XIII

There is something terribly wrong
in the televised images we are being shown.
I am waiting to see a "Hungarian" boy throwing a rock at a tank.
I am waiting to see the South Ossetians
jumping over the barbed wire to freedom (in Berlin).
I was captivated by these images when I was six and eleven.
Now we are the wall builder to the tune of $57 million:
But we want to keep those who would be courageous
and vote with their feet
on the correct side of the wall
(at least a virtual electronic wall).

XIV

The young boy in black and white
had a bandage around his head,
around his blinded eyes.
"It's so dark tonight" he said.
He sat in the wagon seat next to his grandfather
in the shadows of a moonless night.
His grandfather coached the single horse forward,
and the wagon creaked as it rolled westward
in a long procession of people toward the border.
This wasn't a cowboy drama about the American West,
but this movie affected me the rest of my life.
It was about Hungary in 1956
and it ended with the red star being put in place
in the city square.
I thought little of this till I was a music teacher
and met a 'cellist who had carried her cello
through the woods for fifty miles that same night—
toward Austria, toward freedom.

XV

This Guernica of 2008 is testing out
the new Luftwaffe policy of intimidation and force:
and the city has been destroyed again.
There is no 1937 Pablo Picasso still painting now
who will free us from our abstract shame.
The finished mural has finally returned home.

XVI

The army secretary that I know is now on her vacation;
We swim together each afternoon in a week of perfect weather.
I have watched the television broadcasts in disgust.
(The conversion to digital television means those sets
(on government regulated) cable will continue to work,
sending their regulated programming.
Those televisions receiving broadcasts over the "free" airwaves
with an antenna will not.
These will require a coupon from the government
to get a government subsidized (substitute controllable)
black box to allow persons to continue with their old TV sets.
There are television cameras in stores and streets.
The Russians speak doublespeak in the UN Security Council.
But I do not feel informed or secure.
We now only bang the gavel and adjourn our talks
for our tired 9:15 bedtimes.

XVII

I want Reagan back in office to"bang his shoe"
in a cold-war show of power.
I want to pour out my bottled water;
I can no longer drink American Budweiser
But must drink imported foreign beer.

XVIII

The waves lap the shores of many an earthly paradise.
Two flags fly in the breeze in mine;
their flapping punctuates the sound of the waves.
The bottom flag is black with white
and is to remind us of those missing in this current action.
Freedom fighters.

James Ellerston
5:00 a.m.
August 20, 2008

fence wire

a cool breeze blew steadily out of the north west;
the teen-boy son put his foot on the bottom wire
and stretched the woven wire upward,
gnarled hands of the father put on the clamp around the steel;
the man's strength of experience twisted the short wire on the post.
two moved in harmony in their morning task—
fencing this rested land, for the run of angus cattle
in the fall call to forage for the missed left-behind crop.

the heavy cylindrical post driver rang out metallically across the greening field;
it was still spring, rows of corn stretched parallel to the section line fence;
the father had farmed this land as a tenant before
in the good prices after the Second War when he had first married;
the young artistic wife-pianist living in the farm house,
cooking on a wood stove with no toilet, no running water,
straining her small fingers to pick up kindling rather than running arpeggios;
now was the second time he had rented this land hoping for economies of scale,
(after a hopeful trip to Chicago to visit the land-owning aged widow in her hotel suite).

making fence was something the boy could do with his father;
mud clung to the scuffed leather shoes of both
while adolescent feet sweat in heavy cotton stockings;
this was something the two could share in the father's world—
not the boy's mental world of violin lessons, reading Dickens,
struggling with the existential thoughts of Sartre;
the tall boy talked of joining the Navy,
but that the war in Vietnam (Gulf of Tonkin Incident) scared him
and he guessed he'd go to college in a year to become a teacher;
idle talk but meaningful dialogue to the boy;
there were more than the barbs on the top wires between them.

at supper, mother and father talked together about Vietnam on the CBS news;
they said the teen would have their blessing if he went to Canada to live;
they didn't believe in the war anyway; it was a wasted effort, consider the young dead;
just look what it had done to the neighbor boy the dad hired to day work in the fields,
he just wasn't the same after his army years.

the sturdy fence built across the land that day is gone now,
torn-down for today's profitable big agriculture farm operations;
at the widow's death the nearby neighbors bought the fields
hoping for their son's future profitable agri-operation;
his eight-row harvesters now munch through the last yard-line of that farm's horizon;
the wordiness of Dickens still remains in a man's mind who today writes verbose poetry.

James R. Ellerston
July 16, 2014

in remembrance of the Korean enigma:
please explain that "Inchon" thing with the helicopter in the auditorium

there was the quiet inhalation of wind amidst the torrid continuity of life on the apprehensive world stage;
this was not intentional but the industrialized cooling fans on the auditorium platform searchlights
bathed the theater of battle in the rotating sounds of a clouded breathing volatile world—
there was no innocent hope before death came oppressively in a flashing infernal percussive rampage;
the audience was like drafted soldiers passively shipped out by the printed orders on their program into
dawns light and stared blindly ahead sitting stiffly in silence with anticipation for their part in the mission.

there was the quiet sound of peaceful lapping surf rolling gently onto a crucial sodden beachhead;
this so purposeful to the conflicted reality of the barrage of drumming impressing later on embattled minds;
an unseen armada of imagined landing craft rose and fell awkwardly on the breaking swells--
ignored by the murderous composition as thousands dutifully followed their martial orders
vomiting in the boat as the fife piped its playful tune of death's march forced ahead merged
into duet with an innocent crossfire child singing its alto song to the rising tide and crashing sea of men.

the yellow star rose in a pre-planned fair-weather staging dawn of pre-positioned golden spot lights
shining reflections on brass and metal as the rousing fanfare recalled the anguished mental cries
of snared lives cut in half as waves of men fell down to the repeated tap and rap of the mechanized agony--
the first wading ashore were caught in casualty rolls of surf no longer sun-streaked but red-wine stained;
the sound of choppers pounded the very atmosphere with the muscled sound of pulsing manic energy;
calm heads burst like torn drums captured in the deadly insanity of warfare for a righteous cause.

those who would call the bombastic bleeding exercise a tourniquet in halting the fall of domino states
finally drew the 38th line in the sand in a rugged mountainous region of snow-trodden cold war;
here hymn like chords tolled in melodious order represented the thousands who died there—
songful choruses sounded too late for marching the amputated feet of this frozen winter gunfire hell;
the armed-forces radios of sliding trombones belted out big band swing to drown out boyish pulse of fear;
as bombardiers released their rack of whistling death to burst the bloodied eardrums targeted below.

newly introduced into the battlefield the pulsating blades of the whirly-bird earned its rank for MASH;
oriented patterns of shadows swirled the arena stimulating searching eyes seeking flight or survival--
while amid the constant high tension barrage of repeated bombing sacrifice for the greater band occurred;
operations came to an armistice finale and the fife and drums led nations to an acceptable united solution;
at the conclusion blood red seas washed our traumatic memories and cleansed our wounded conscience;
a wailing flute exhaled an alto dirge raised for the bloated belly of a child lying dead on the sand.

Performance of "Inchon" by Robert W. Smith
By the ICCC Concert Band Friday April 24, 2009
Paul Bloomquist, Director
Poem by James R. Ellerston
April 28, 2009
Revision May 1, 2009

(Israel Blockades Gaza Killing an American On A Supply Ship)
A Short Memory Forgets 1943, 1948, 1967, 2010

A short memory forgets in Israel
the desire to be free and found a homeland nation
while ships off-shore blockade a seacoast
yesterday and yet today;
There is a lack of freedom to choose one's life
when religious difference creates suspicion between—
and Muslim, Jew, and Christian meet
after the results of past warfare have yielded power—
giving a need for new recognition of a situation
as defenders of each are armed
and people are walled off from one another.

Both sides are survivors of years of warfare;
Both fear unjust bombs and rockets;
Both are now fleeing persons expelled from home;
An "iron curtain" again descends with concrete walls
stretching across the endless barricaded arid lands
and razor wire is the new weapon of separation—
showing lack of toleration of others' freedoms—
as identity papers are checked
and policed at countless military checkpoints
and borders are controlled by racial profiling.

There is more need for humanitarian aid
not more military in the streets
as persons are killed by bombs, bus, and car
attempting horrific enforcement of claims on territory;
The continual urban battles
result in walled ghettos in cities—
as desired genocide seeks a contemporary solution—
against today's resistance fighters on both sides
coming of age and ideals in refugee camps
and new settlements in war-occupied lands.

The cry "This is our Land, our Home"
is not proven by settlement of conquered territories
and the blindness of not seeing fellow human beings
but only seeing people as different than me;
Proudly a national flag waves above each
despite the lack of material needs of both—
and the desire to eradicate each other
creates a ripple of international tension across the globe..

A Balfour Declaration was made in 1917
and a Protectorate was made and expired
for imperial European powers of occupation
as a League of Nations searched for a Mandate solution
and Palestinians were subject to a dispossession and sale of their lands
as progress was desired and worked for through peace and warfare—
and evil men at Wannsee sought only The Final Solution—
so that afterwards a United Nations searched for a resolution
of several peoples right to exist and survive in the same land,
through decades of Accords and Agreements—
the interventions of countless United States Presidents..
Meanwhile the Warsaw Ghetto walled off the Jews awaiting certain death;
Meanwhile the British blockaded the Jewish ships
bringing newly declared "illegal" immigrants to found Israel;
Meanwhile the Israelis now build barricades
and blockade the supply ships of the Palestinians of Gaza.

In reality religion and race still divide the lands of the Middle East.
Israel was founded, armed, and protected
by Jews fleeing the deadly past of European prejudice
who were now willing to fight all who opposed them—
Ottoman, French, British, Arab, even American;
Palestinians were already at home in the Middle East Protectorates
during the scattering Jewish Diaspora across the many nations
and farmed the dry desert under occupiers for thousands of years;
The world waited for a resolution in 1948 and still watches now—
while Palestine yet awaits nationhood and borders—
and the sovereign rights of all individuals deserve recognition;
Nightly news reports that ships still try passing through
another current coastal blockade off the desert shores;
In this explosive region where cultures merge
defiant people are being unjustly killed by hate
as bullets still fly and powder bursts
onboard supply ships and almost daily in the streets.

June 5-6, 2010
James R. Ellerston

Encore Singers on Another Pearl Harbor Day

I find myself again in the auditorium orchestra pit, instrument in hand,
after a year which gave me titanium and plastic knees;
A little older sitting before the music page lit by the glare of light,
its white and black abstraction giving me the privilege of taking part;
I draw bow on string and my sound mixed with others
makes music and is sent out to be received.

There are some songs which always make me choke and tear;
and tonight the young singers and dancers perform one of them again;
(A melody which defines "home" and America to the world;)
We celebrate this tune today in rehearsal this December 7, 2010.
The young nineteen-year-olds dance and sing with youth and joy.
We get to "White Christmas" and the tempo is dance-ably fast
when compared to that sung by the great Bing Crosby in 1941;
The first broadcast was on Christmas Day after the "Day of Infamy";
Soon millions were drafted and heard the song their first time
on far flung Pacific islands far away from home.
Heard the version Bing recorded in just 18 minutes on May 29, 1942.
(The record was released unbelievably in the summer on July 30th!)

This was back in the days of the old 78 rpm records;
and by October the song spent eleven weeks on the hit parade;
It resonated with listeners during World War II;
The Armed Forces Radio Network was flooded with requests
from young people fighting far from home and family.
Into the days of 33 rpm vinyl, 8-track, and cassettes the song endured
and according to Guinness, crooner Bing sold over 50 million recordings;
(A little surprising for a song about people desiring cold and snow:)
The rarely sung beginning original verse concludes:
"But it's December the twenty-fourth--
And I am longing to be up North."

April 30, 1975 the Armed Forces Radio in Saigon
repeatedly began playing the song shortly after ten a.m.;
The recording was broadcast as part of a secret, pre-arranged plan
precipitating the U.S. Evacuation of Saigon;
This regular repetition of Irving Berlin's "White Christmas"
was the signal for American personnel to move immediately
to the evacuation points ending American involvement in Vietnam.
There was no white snow and not enough helicopters for all who wished to go;
Some waiting on rooftops unfortunately reached for an empty sky;
and many were left behind to die in what was the final tragedy of the war.

Sing tonight for all those veterans, and those away from home;
for young people in distant lands and on ships at sea,
Sing tonight for those who with a few easy words and the magic of music
might be transported however briefly with a few thoughts of home.
One lyricist in changing the words of the usually unsung verse
somehow wrote of every person's reality;
(The Keane version expressed universal melancholy:)
"The sun's been hiding, the streets are gray,
the rain has been falling down...
It reminds me each time I roamed
I'm longing to be back home."

December 7, 2010
James R. Ellerston

No Armistice This Time!

A 'copter went down in Afghanistan,
The cargo was thirty-one men;
Mass-produced coffins were hidden with American flags
To honor young men who on foreign shores had suddenly died;
Fighting the terrorists who threaten our lives—
      With car-bombs and buildings blown high.

The Turks controlled Persia for nearly three-hundred years;
Then British and French held their Palatine mandates;
The Durand borders were drawn and countries created
Without provision for getting along;
The Treaty of Versailles moved masses of people—it was wrong.

The Afghans were fought over by the British
Who brought with them their government and faith;
Then a Second World War made the fight for control—
      continue for decades ahead.
Oil the prize made for targets of greed—
      Mid-east land was to be the prize,
This they all fought for over time—
      thinking the battle could be won.

A 'copter went down in Afghanistan;
That dreaded knock pounded thirty-one doors;
There were thirty-one families with grief shattered hearts,
Where dreams of shared children and lives were no more.
Thirty-one coffins in a cargo-plane's hold
      were flown flag-covered to America's shores.

We treatied-away the once proud land of Kurdistan—
      And now the persecuted Kurds have no where to go;
We created the countries of Iraq and Iran
      with deep divisions and troubles to soar.
Even the Nazi's were after south-central-Asian crude
      While the British like despots did rule;
Propped up by Americans later dictators ruled with fear—
      Educating people that force might make right—
      With no form of democracy in sight.

The Soviets oppressed and played their Afghan war games,
Without success their troops were killed and were maimed;
Mechanized warfare didn't work in hidden mountain caves;
The dead and the dying were sent northward home—
Mourning families filled Moscow
      with the withdrawal pleas of the brave.

A 'copter went down in Afghanistan
Those brave Navy SEALS met their deaths;
Some nation made money supplying the rocket-grenades
That lined up those thirty-one pairs of boots—
      Along with rifles and dog-tags and helmets—
To commemorate their way to their graves.

The Russians packed up and too late they went home,
The U.S. backed Taliban over Russia had won;
The Soviet system fell and the Reagan years went swell—
      The undercover CIA deed was done;
The whole operation was soon forgotten until twenty years later
      The day of the Taliban albatross had come.

The U.S. quick found an enemy the boys with guns could die for;
The Twin Towers in Manhattan came crashing down;
      Pennsylvania people in a plane died heroes that day;
An airplane hit the Pentagon and Representatives
      In our most political town—
      had to have their own say.
And the President told the nation that a serious time had come:
We would fight once again in the Ottoman Empire—
      Until the Great War task this time was done.

A 'copter went down in Afghanistan;
The cargo was thirty-one brave men;
Mass-produced coffins were shrouded with flags
To honor those young men who on foreign shores had suddenly died
While fighting the terrorists who threaten our lives—
        With car bombs and buildings blown high.

It's now America's longest war—
        if you count fighting on all of its fronts;
The embassies felled in Africa, the trains blown up in Spain.
We are fighting on fronts in Iraq and Iran,
        and must add Afghanistan again;
We finally invaded Pakistan and SEALS shot Bin Laden dead—
        And the body-bags continued to pile
        and to be enshrined with flags;
But the President in Washington waves the red, white, and blue,
        And after a decade still doesn't have the courage
        to bring the troops home before more are dead instead.

But what have we learned about a sovereign nation's rights—
        Who should fight in its own civil war?
We arm both sides, profit from sales, and promise to ship them more;
In the name of NATO we form coalitions so the international court will say
        Our invasion in Libya seems legal—
        So plan your war and get there and fight today.
But from Vietnam to Afghanistan we fail to get the message:
Go home America, invade us no more—
        Our fighting should have sent you the signal,
        Corporate America--you'll have a tough time in store.

Will we now follow this hard learned lesson in Libya,
Now that Khadafy is hopefully in power no more?
Can we see that the Rebel Forces on the ground have really done it alone
(With help from air-strikes by friendly NATO in a timely show of force,)
Without invading United States troops based on the ground—
        No armada of landing-craft welcomed ashore.

A 'copter went down in Afghanistan,
  There were thirty-one comrades remembered and grieved.
Thirty-one services and funerals of death
  And names on markers of thirty-one graves—
  With prayers that personal faith saves.
There are thirty-one places at family tables now empty
  Of the thirty-one souls who gave all;
There are thirty-one lives now gone leaving a void—
Thirty-one won't be home to say goodnight
  to their children down the hall.

A 'copter went down in Afghanistan
The cargo was thirty-one men;
Mass-produced coffins are hidden with flags;
There are thirty-one more places at family tables now empty
  Of the thirty-one souls who freely gave all;
This should influence graying aged politicians—
  building Washington careers on the Capitol Mall.

There are people in Washington who still believe in warfare fables;
The nation cried and mourned—
No terrorist will ever attack us again;
But the I.E.D.'s continued to explode
And the bodies are shipped home.

A 'copter went down in Afghanistan
There are thirty-one comrades remembered and grieved;
There are thirty-one emptied places at home kitchen tables;
There were thirty-one men responding to their countries call;
  (So let's take 31 seconds to repost this to all.)

Inspired by a posting by Joyce M. Justice on Facebook Aug. 7, 2011
Poetry by James R. Ellerston
August 20-22, 2011.

Veterans Day 2011: Not Knowing You Had Needed To Step So Carefully

I.

I find a table in the student center snack bar
behind rows of blue chairs set in graveyard rows to dignify the occasion;
The brass band opens the program with rhythmic music;
A chorus of celebrants gathers in various student daily costume
upon stepped risers to focus their unified sound;
Friday's weekly-beards cover young boyish unshaven faces;
Students amble in seeking chairs
Their eyes still in a stupor from their morning classes;
Absent are the martial drums of parading troops
as the Colors are presented by soldiers in camouflage fatigues;
More students group-up out of curiosity on the shoulders of the crowd.

The man on the platform and the band try to lead us in the national anthem;
The man doesn't sing and oddly neither does the choir on the stepped risers;
The crowd is oddly silent but attentive;
By the time we "gave proof through the night that our flag was still there"
the choir had begun to resound to the gestures of the choral master;
But the chorus did sing out the question "Who are the Brave?"
beginning with men's voices and the heralding trumpets of the brass.
The dignity of the circumstances are regained on the front-line.

The college president speaks of his role in Operation Iraqi Freedom—
the valor that defines warriors includes those who have returned home
having been changed forever by their experiences;
He breaks down as he describes coming back from Iraq on two weeks break —
and he talks not of the battle horrors in warfare on deployment —
yet tries to speak of the kindness shown to those deployed
upon their homeward leave;
(Airline passengers had given-up their seats to the boys returning home);
He weeps again from his thanksgiving,
but he has the students' attention in respectful silence at his genuine being,
and he pushes his way onward across the battleground of his speech,
reciting statistics of those wounded or killed as casualties in current wars.
In the end he talks of the number of homeless veterans—
He talks of those unable to carry on their lives in a productive way—
To those who might be pacifists after our experiences carrying banners
and parading during the later Vietnam-era;
The college president issues the moral challenge:

The feeling that nothing is worth fighting for in a war—
is worse than war itself.
Pacifists 0, those who fight for us 1.

Within this group of gathered people a call goes out for veterans to rise,
and one young man rises amid the sea of chairs;
(Veterans are across town at the Catholic high school event);
Next is a choral reading by an oral interpretation class
relating our event to the post days of Nine-Eleven (2001);
It is a litany of ideas about being American
and is more of meaning to those performing than those straining to listen
amid the background noise of students passing through the space
and the refrigeration equipment humming away in the snack bar.
There is more parade music from the brass band
as the dignitaries leave the platform in battle field survival instinct,
their dignity intact.
Students resume their homework at the tables,
and I glance through the newspaper of veterans' profiles—
One page in particular catches my eye.

II.

 I had always rushed into your shop
concerned with my own haste,
concerned with my own business,
concerned with my own young life
and found you very slow moving and exact.
I found you patiently explaining details
to each of the customers in line before me;
I found you very methodical in following each procedure
with each of the technical machines you used in your work.
Sometimes I thought you seemed so distracted.
Sometimes I thought you were rigid with design ideas
(I was always in such a hurry).

Today I glanced through a newspaper lying on a table and
I found that you were still alive
because you had worked carefully without haste;
I found that you were still alive
because you tended to the business at hand—
That you were once young and eager

and responsible for other young lives beside your own—
That there was a reason for your very methodical mode of movement.

You are the successful Vietnam Veteran
that I never knew was in any war;
You had moved along the jungle trail and dusty roads
avoiding enemy explosive devices;
trying to draw out enemy fire with your body
so the big guns could have their way.
(You might as well have had a job in the Marines defusing mines).
One of these devices had exploded under you;
(Did it damage your hearing?
Is that the reason for the quizzical look on your face as I rattled hurriedly on?)
Your life depended on your being careful and methodical.
You received the Purple Heart.

When you returned stateside to a campus world of shouting war protests,
you still had to learn to keep you head down from the violence
and be silent in your inner world of real war experiences—
while others held candles and sang songs with acoustic guitars,
and thought they knew how to fight about what was good for peace,
(in a world of politics, nationalism, colonialism, and cold-war doctrine;)
Campus disruptions nation-wide included the infamous battle-ground Kent State.
Now you have a right to be focused on your own inner world of peace;
while others rattle-off reams of rapid-fire words in their daily haste;
Now you have the right to have your hand shake and rattle the crisp paper
as you hold the brown bag for my purchase at your counter;.
Today I glanced through the newspaper printed for Veterans Day
and realized I was terribly ignorant of your past life—
Not knowing you had worn wet leather boots in the explosive-laden jungle
and bamboo-spiked rice paddies in South-east Asia—
Not knowing you had learned the life-lessons of survival in a real war;
Not knowing you had needed to step so carefully.

November 11, 2011
James R. Ellerston

For Raoul Wallenberg: Born 1912, Date of death unknown

An accident of wealthy propertied and moneyed birth
might have made You just another spoiled rich kid
of your Swedish industrial family selling armaments to the world,
instead You came to America and saw its life,
and earned a degree at the University of Michigan.

You became the belated consciousness of the war torn world
in the final weeks, days and hours of the Holocaust
in your adopted Hungary;
You were able to convince the enemy to guard and protect
those innocents who became your chosen people.

As a protected Swedish diplomat in Budapest
You might have lived an easy life of fine dining and parties
but instead set up food pantries for the outcast,
the starving and beaten down;
flour and bread became the currency of life;
the steam engines and cattle cars from Budapest to Auschwitz stopped.

You might have chosen to hide in blind innocence
behind your country's neutral Swedish banner,
but instead defiantly hung that blue and yellow flag and its passports
over lives You had never met and yet sought to protect;
You convinced the weak and stragglers that living was a possibility.

You might have chosen to avoid danger
but instead You went to the most dangerous points
of genocidal conflict between Jew and Nazi,
between those in power and those stripped of power;
You immediately saved lives on exhausting death marches
and in the squalid undefended walled-in ghetto prison.

You did not accept the powers of evil in the Nazi world
but instead stared persons such as Eichmann in the face,
and threatened Nazis with future judicial War Crimes consequences;
You bent their actions away from their horrific paths—
if even for one day at a time;
In all you spared 100,000 human beings from certain death.

You were unable to defend your righteous actions of selfless goodness,
in the face of terrible deadly wrong
against the henchman of the Stalinist system
when the car stopped and the dreaded knock came on your door
and You were arrested by the Red Army on January 17, 1945;
You probably spent your final years traveling the Siberian horrors
and the deprivation of the Soviet Gulag.

You have received the second Honorary Citizenship
granted by the United States in the year 1981
and have been nominated for a Congressional Gold Medal
in the hundredth anniversary year of your birth in 2012;
amongst the many honors of grateful nations.

A grateful world has built monuments in your name
(they sprout in cities and on college campuses)
to remind all that in the bitter hour of lost hope,
one man can make a difference in the world—
in the contest between man's goodness and his potential to do wrong.

Your memory is owed an end date on your many memorials,
and the descendents of those you personally saved
by your simple brave signature
finally deserve to know the probable details
of your desolate and isolated death;
The pressure of many embassies may bring forth this Russian knowledge.

Your just cause springs forth eternal
when the nations of the world have not yet eliminated the genocide
against which you personally and courageously fought;
but many continue to be inspired by your angelic name
to lift united voices in that same battle here on earth.

James R. Ellerston
February 8, 2012

2012: Needed— A Flower in a Gun Barrel

Forty-two years ago the white bed sheet hugged the bricks and fluttered in the wind;
Black paint in awkward characters loudly shouted out unjust youths' untimely deaths';
I gawked at it draped from our Student Union hanging troubled in fading afternoon sun;
Grabbing my vision in struggle— beginning an internal hunger and ceaseless weeping—
It proclaimed an anguished painful truth that May 4th day into our tranquil city of refuge.

Thirteen seconds of volleys were aimed at the merely weak and classmates passing-by—
At Kent State blunt force triumphed over the power of flowers causing US eternal shame;
Blossoms were pushed into a rifle barrel from the young woman's hand and gentle heart;
Socially conscious and uninvolved casual bystanders both felt the bullets heated wrath;
Over-the-top firepower was used unjustly in an attempt to regain righteous social control.

Directing governors were elders who feared the free speech and assembly of angry youth:
There were the young irate and political who studied daily military propaganda events;
There were young men scared of the draft-lottery received that previous chilling autumn;
There were students not wishing to fight in the butchering entanglements of foreign wars.
(The young Ohio National Guard men possibly were afraid for their personal safety also.)

Years later, not having learned from our past, our youth still meet bullets on city streets;
All we have been able to do is proclaim a Registered Historic Place on an Ohio campus
Where once blood of innocents spread across the crumbling asphalt and cracked concrete.
We placed a memorial sculpture of Abraham poising society's knife over innocent Isaac
But at a less controversial location far away on a different university campus (Princeton).

The symbolic white purity of the wafting cotton shroud invoking our belated involvement
Still is etched sunlit in non-fading memory in my white-haired but-still-conflicted mind;
And anguished horror from gruesome black letters so hurriedly starkly outlined provoked
Is nightly announced from the prompters on the network puppet news with vivid images
Dramatizing regret for our traumatized soldiers home from ugly fronts in robotic wars.

James R. Ellerston
March 26, 2012

V.

The muffler rattles in the Ford car as it idles in the unloading zone;
we also are taking Delta Airlines;
The sign tells us where to get out next to the concrete barricade.
The young man in camouflage swings a full-packed duffle from the trunk;
 he lowers it to the ground.
The woman, older and shorter, than the young man
gets out of the driver's door of the car with the self-imposed care
of a person aging daily—she looks like a mother;
The man, with the muscles of a disciplined and well-trained youth
walks along the rear of the car toward her;
he mumbles something to her.
He quickly turns and in the same motion picks up the duffle
and swings it onto his back—
and with the same decisiveness steps away.
The woman stands there—
frozen in temporal agony—
then moves back to the driver's door and swings it easily open,
getting in and pulling the car into gear in one motion.
In the brief instant that the young soldier turned,
I saw a tear slide down his smooth black cheek.
The sign on the barricade proclaimed a three-minute limit
for something in life so agonizing to both.

VI.

Just behind them in the airport drop-off zone
we had gotten out of the red car belonging to our daughter's boyfriend;
(She had taken the full day off from work to drive us to the airport)
Within three minutes our luggage was out of the trunk
and we had again crossed the temporal barricade of concrete
that often exists between child and parents,
or brother and sister.
But I called my daughter back for one more hug in the Philadelphia air,
our moment filled with the exhaust from hundreds of cars
and dozens of vans claiming to be airport limousines.
We turned apart, and I slowly looked back;
her left-turn blinker was already on and she pulled-out
with confidence into the busy lane of city traffic.

XI.

Groups of young soldiers wait at the airport gates for announcements;
it is hard to know which way their flights are going.
They inquire at the busy information desks
and move with the easy confidence of athletic young men
dressed in camouflage and suede leather boots;
Many have sun-tanned skin from drills.
Their eyes look straight ahead.

Most travelers on January 3rd are heading home from holidays
with friends and family and seasonal parties;
The young men and women in uniform wear the confusion
of leaving the family of their birth
to return to the even closer knit family of their unit.
There will be little "horsing-around" as they are deployed again
into the vast spaces of the Afghanistan wasteland.
They will not need to do anything but survive
the next few months of actual warfare.
There is mental-tension in all as their gate at the airport is reassigned
and they march off as a group.

The Tragedy of Northern Ireland (for David Drissel)

It was a giants' cause that was the erupted stony way in the volcanic beginning,
rising steeply abrupt from the pounding surf with rocky footprint shores;
She climbed white cliffs of innocent purity to meadows green with abundant arbors;
but a bloody wrath of conquering invaders destroyed this idyllic Eden
        and brought the plundering Norman Orange to this periled nation.
William's victory in the Battle of Boyne seared the year 1690 into Irish consciousness.

Heroes and martyrs of past and present world-wide and within depict Ireland's struggle;
Presently sprayed and brushed in murals and graffiti are Belfast's emblazoned buildings,
 with harsh political advertisements for causes and coexistence in a divided homeland;
The symbolic Red Hand of Ulster has swept in bloody vengeance a stormy swath,
        a horde of shootings and bombings across this battered land,
standing now divided by physical walls, peace-lines, gates, and interface areas,

Today's Catholics and Protestant brethren live in sequestered neighborhoods,
where youth behind the barricades are carefully taught the lessons of separation,
        prejudicial hate, and curiosity about their rivals for control of the state.
Politics can turn bloody here in the commemorations of Boyne on July 12th,
as marchers in colorful clad opposition claim the streets,
        and roughly prescribe the territories of harsh gang surveys,
fighting bitterly to dispute their rival lots in life.

For endless centuries onward the green-clovered fields rose above the sea
        providing sustenance to those of faith and ambition;
Like a colony your abundant feed grains were taxed away
        to sustain the teeming population multitudes of English urban industry;
Your hungered stomach famished in its thirst for freedom;
The fruit of your earth was blighted by the English occupation
        which tried to purposely starve the populace and quench the thirst for liberty.
The fungus of superiority and implied inferior servitude
        caused one million to hunger toward death and burial.

Softly saddened the lilting magic of your weeping Celtic song
        and the quick snap of dance rhythm diversion
kept the spirits of the dying generations in beauty and life.
Irish families produced more plentiful babies
        than your land was able to suckle at conquered exhausted breasts;
Walls of emigrants left your sheltering shores
        in a departure of the desperate and ambitious for unknown harbors
Finding life in an Irish Diaspora in diseased tenements, mines, railroads and farms;
        Irish people built enclaves on America's shores one million strong.

Celtic-Gaelic language and literature and colorful costumes,
        long bitterly suppressed by arrogant English conquerors,
Still live alongside your imposed grammatical tongue.
(You had a forced early start learning today's international language,
        the language of business and computers which has enveloped the earth.

Your birth as a free but divided nation which was forcibly aborted in 1916,
was again stillborn in 1921 from a violent rising up in the last century's wake of tears.
The Easter Monday Rising of 1916 failed in its military objective at the Post Office,
        in its attempt to overthrow external rule;
Michael Collins, a martyr at the unfulfilled age of 31 did succeed in birthing
        the controversy of the Irish Free State in the south,
which didn't pass through its tormented adolescence until 1949,
        when today's Republic of Ireland was proclaimed a sovereign adult
        in the world family of independent nations;
But the divorce from your children in Northern Ireland
        continued with custodial battlegrounds of strife.

 Fifty years of ethno-political socio-economic conflict for equal civil rights
continues to cause battle-lines between nationalists
        who want all Irish in the same republican family of independents,
And the Protestant Unionists who want the northern counties
        to belong to the United Kingdom family parented by the English Queen;
brings out fighting which has invoked violent armed British military intervention
        to protect Northern Irish citizens holding U.K. passports.
Bloody Sundays followed by over a month's worth of Bloody Fridays
        has led to the ultimate deaths of over three thousand innocents and armed.

Commemorations of the agonizing gnawing hunger strike of Bobby Sands,
        an elected MP and IRA activist held in the jowls of empty bowels and bladder,
Who was squeezed in the famine steel grip of policy by the Iron Lady,
        are still a provocation for "moaning" and low-level violence.
The veneration of insurgents from the past is a smoldering funeral pyre of the Irish soul,
        spewing hot ash over the consciousness of the nation
        where so many followed destiny to prison, death, and grave.
Monuments to Irishmen and those around the world pock the troubled landscape.

Today in this land of concrete barricades and high wire fences
        which segregate peoples into ghetto neighborhoods and safe-zones
Sect allegiances can be set aside in locations of free-association by today's youth;
Young men culturally united by their athletic interest ride their skateboards
        in a taught balancing act over the crumbling edges of the divided territories,
traveling over the cemented bumps and obstacles—
        To a freer exhibition and communication,
        To a new interpretation of sectarian pasts apart,
        To building friendships by association in this sport of youthful daring.

Walls and high fences may keep the home-built firebombs of hot-headed rival factions
        from crossing into neighborhoods wrongly seen as opposition,
But the polished ball bearings, jive slogans, and young men's agility while they interact
        may roll out a smoothly paved model for a future
        moving toward cross-sectarian friendships
and provide hopeful optimism across the future barricades which divide all Irish.

James Ellerston, May 29, 2012

1912-2012: Down by the Bow Until She Sank (Defying Nature)

She was good for the economy of vast numbers of hungry urban workers;
She launched in Belfast the pride of Irish shipbuilding technology,
the creation of a swarming sweating Irish labor force;
She crewed-up in Southampton with the unemployed and desperate for work;
Eight men had died before her keel slipped her dry-dock
and became hazardously seaborne.
Outfitted with the grandest of luxuries
She attracted the most wealthy in an age of industrial prosperity.
The bowels of her steerage were filled with innocent emigrants
sailing and dreaming toward a new life of golden prosperity.

Her Marconi wireless was pre-occupied with the pleasure greetings of the leisured,
and its operator failed to send the last fateful ice warning
to the searching eyes of the bridge.
The lookouts called in agony at the appearance and size of the iceberg;
Last minute attempts to alter course
could not swing her endangered bow-side away from that cold submerged danger;
Frozen force plowed a furrow through iron plate and popping rivets;
Her starboard side was torn open by that icy berg,
crucifying the unsinkable idea in design flaw,
as if again the side of the Son's body was rent open by the Roman spear;
In pain she twisted and moaned and her safety bulkheads buckled,
and her hull plummeted to a deep and dark watery grave
as the Marconi radioed out a repeated call of "CQD" for assistance.

With her death came a century's wail of pain:
From those in frigid water uttering final screams and groans
floundering within death's drowning freezing grip;
From those in life boats lowered in haste, panic and strokes of luck
to survive a Carpathian rescue from the Atlantic's grasp;
The agony of those trapped below decks
with no hope of escaping awash in ocean's froth;
The cries that have sounded now for one hundred years
criticize man's brashness against Nature's power
and the sea's relentless vindication over blind pride.
April 15, 1912 was the crucifixion of an idea—
That man could build supreme against seaward wrath—
and that a redundancy of safety systems could provide security.

The Information Age and the Individulation of Statistics:
IBM and its Hollerith Machines in World War II

They had ridden cramped in the train together,
urine running down their legs;
the smell of uncontrollable defecation burning the nose
as they stood for days in the stench of the rail car,
where they were hurried both in and out by snarling dogs.

Forced cruel separation upon arrival from her husband and son,
she had to survive the next judgement
where the elderly and children to weak to work went to the smokestacks,
by calling out "I can type".
She was motioned to go with the living.

She found herself working in the bright light of an office,
a room full of women working with the whir and chatter
of IBM's rented out Hollerith punch-card machines;
Daily she answered the telephone,
"Extension 4496, *Hollerith-Büro*."

Daily as the trains arrived she entered the names
and the tattoo numbers to ID the cards,
and of course the code for *Juden*, a simple 8, or Gypsies, a simple 12;
There were codes for everything,
including Auschwitz, 001.

She had seen her husband and oldest son only once again,
and she memorized the five-digit numbers
cruelly burned in purple ink into the thin tissue of their arms;
She had seen them at the fence separating the men's' and women's camp.
and passed a near-sacred crust of bread to the emaciated little boy.

The five-digit numbers were used on the IBM cards once again—
to record in German precision the mode of death of the millions.
She punched into the stiff paper cards the code for execution D4,
suicide E5, or *(SB) Sonderbehandlung* ("special treatment, gas chamber) F6.
(Where did you think they got all those records of who died at Auschwitz, 001?)

Each day she punched away at her machine in data-entry
until the day she absent-mindedly punched those memorized tattoos
into those nifty hole-filled information carriers followed by the code F6.
In her wails of grief and agony she was led away and went up the chimneys,
added to the day's quota of soot and smoke.

Most evidence of IBM's operation at Auschwitz was ultimately
destroyed by Red Army bombardment and Nazi demolition.
Mistakenly surviving is the telephone directory for the Auschwitz extention
where she so bravely answered the phone in a "survivors tone".
IBM most likely evacuated their Hollerith rental machines.

After the war on Europe's *Juden* had ended and the camps disbanded
IBM filed for war reparations for the loss of some of their machines in camps,
(After all the machines were only rented and still belonged to IBM in Europe).
Not legally tried in any U.S. court of international tribunal for genocide or treason,
IBM's directors escaped the specter of Nuremburg altogether until "the book".

IBM to the current day declines comment or the opening of its cramped files,
either on military inventory management for the *Wehrmacht*
or their proven guilt in the genocide of the Six Million.
The real corporate account books would have a book keeper's precision
on scales balancing greed and guilt with a lack of humanity.

Auschwitz 001, *Buchenwald* 002, *Dachau* 003, *Flossenburg* 004, *Groß-Rosen* 005
Herzogenbusch 006, *Mauthausen* 007, *Natzweiler* 008, *Neuengamme* 009
Ravensbrück 010, *Sachsenhausen* 011, *Stuthof* 012;
Released A 1, Transfer B 2, Died C 3, Execution D 4, Suicide E 5,
(SB) Senderbehandlung (Special treatment, Gas Chamber) F 6, Escape G 7.

James R. Ellerston
April 12, 2012
with credits to Edwin Black, IBM and the Holocaust, Expanded Edition 2012

I Remember Buying LEGOS (Twenty-Four Years Later 1988-2012)

There is a man I hope still living who was once a young boy in Hungary in 1988;
He lived by the Romanian border with his family—
A mother and his father who had coal-black hair and big pleading brown eyes;
The father thrust the money into my outstretched hands with trust and anguish;
He was not allowed to shop in the Intourist store in his own communist Hungary;
He had worked hard in the black market economy earning illegal foreign currency;
His Austrian Schillings and West German Marks would be accepted in the store—
accompanied by my own Passport number to purchase his son a LEGO Pirate Set.

We had come through the Iron Curtain at the Hungarian border from Austria;
Our coach sat parked under the eyes of the guard-manned watchtowers
which rose above the parallel wire fences stretching endless toward the horizon;
The rear seats of cars in the lane next to us were being removed for inspection;
The hard-faced uniformed young soldier came on the bus staring into each of us;
We timidly held up our Passport for his officious glance and compulsory stamp;
We all had the required Tourist Visa to enter the country for just one day—
to spend our time in Sopron and see the Esterházy palace where Haydn worked.

The guide on the bus said it was alright to do this for the blond-haired mother,
the black-haired father, and the growing Slavic-looking dark-skinned son;
I entered the shop with bravura and boasted in my voice the origins of the cash and
the matronly women at the counter wrapped my purchase in a coarse brown paper;
I spun from the counter glimpsing two soldiers with weapons through the window;
Shouting "Nicht!" at the supervising travel guide and family I proceeded out;
Nearly bumping into the two patrolling guards I walked briskly taking photos—
To hide my nervousness I tried to appear to be the ordinary tourist on a stroll.

Keeping their distance the guide and the family followed me up the street;
I saw a gate between two buildings and entered a courtyard off the main street;
The family followed me in and I gave them possession of their LEGO package
and also the few bills and coins I had received as change in Hungarian Forints;
I received their thanks in broken hesitant English and I wished them well—
I told them "I hoped things would be better for them under Mikhail Gorbachev";
It was impossible to exchange names or addresses with them for security reasons—
but they did have my passport number in the wrapped package of LEGOS.

A man who was once a young boy in Hungary lived by the Romanian border;
His father's coal-black hair and pleading brown eyes begged on behalf of his son;
Fourteen months after I met them the Wall and the Iron Curtain came freely down:
The border was open, streets were unguarded, and LEGOS were available to all.

June 17th, 2012

Anne Frank Began Her Diary Seventy Years Ago

June 20, 1942 a beginning in her own birthday present preserved;
A pen in cursive German script across the page;
Thoughts secreted away in a red plaid notebook;
Hiding away in the upper floors above a shop;
The swinging bookcase secreting the entrance from the world;
The freedom of the toilet only at night;
Hushed voices and softened steps through out one's adolescence;
Fear and terror at unexpected noises or voices down below;
Unexpected love and expression beneath the attic skylight;
The invasive end and ruin of their civilized lives;
Pages scattered on the floor in haste and later gathered up;
Thoughts once censored are now preserved and presented in raw beauty;
A girl with a chance of becoming a woman to be remembered for eternal time;
Mere writings of daily thoughts immortalized and close to sacred for humankind.

James R. Ellerston
June 20, 2012

If Only For The Key

If I had the key there would have been no tragedy of tiny bodies in a bloody mound;
If I had the key after Aurora, plans for law changes would have been found;
If I had the key no fearful child would ever ask, "What is that popping sound?"
If I had the key, the children's school in Newtown would have been the safest place around.

If I had the key those eager children would be out for recess now having fun;
If I had the key there wouldn't be victims of a crazed young man with a high clip gun;
If I had the key, the country would have a new plan enacted with tomorrows dawning sun;
If I had the key the guilt of doing nothing would not stop children who play, skip and run.

If I had the key we would know how to turn the clock of evil times safely back;
If I had the key they wouldn't be making students a bullet proof pink backpack;
If I had the key we wouldn't see adds for bullet proof blankets that fit children like a sack;
If I had the key small angels wouldn't be hidden in closets huddling in a shivering pack.

If I had the key our health plans would improve mental illness care at its core;
If I had the key we could comfort all mourning families whose tears now flood and pour;
If I had the key assault gun sales in troubled times would be allowed no more;
If I'd only had the key, I might have locked my classroom door.

James R. Ellerston
December 20, 2012

The Weiße Rose (The student resistance against Hitler)
München 1.July. 2013 am Geschwister-Scholl Platz 14.15

"Don't step on that," my inner voice cried out
at the casual placement of student's style shod feet on near-sacred words
offending me in its lack of reverence and careless manner
for the ideals on facsimile documents and photographs
embedded in the concrete memorial plaza outside the university hall;
inside are memorial bronze busts and plaques, a vase holding a white rose.

before Hans and Sophie had always placed self-written pamphlets carefully
until Sophie emptied her final challenge from the battered suitcase
over the stone balustrade dumping resistance in the entrance foyer,
papers fluttering two stories below on floors for students' gaze
(before the building janitor saw all with prosecuting eyes)
leading to treacherous responses invoking the Gestapo's gnarled wrath.

five courts were held for the twenty-nine defendants without justice served;
cruel sharp guillotine's blade dropped on brave necks of the initial three—
swiftly martyred Christoph, Hans, and Sophie with their perpetual challenge
to those living to fight for ideals of free thought, speech, and press
and battle against tyranny in its most deadly game without regret
taking the risk, not betraying friends, working toward true democracy.

James R. Ellerston
July 27, 2013

Kristallnacht at 75 years: November 9-10, 1938- 2013

now lies beneath brass inscription such an inadequate marker stone
in mere unkempt square meters of German grass alone,
this decaying monument to painful events for which we moan,
near today's full parking lot of cars— for the *pogrom* can hardly atone.

forgotten memories once had been full lot of garden park
once a time when faithful *Juden* of hallowed synagogue made their mark,
a building and a people sent away in flame and cinder dark,
the *aktion* extinguishing the congregation of believers – their deaths severely stark.

branded by hardened sounds of hateful heels on cobblestone pavement,
again heckled by the street-lining citizens gaping amusement,
their doors knocked on in night's middle and darkened hours' defilement,
these men paraded through streets of commerce without human entitlement.

dripping shards of shattered liquid glass, swept away, in evening's dim lamp,
anguished torching of a synagogue to ashen ruin without firemen's damp,
harsh marching-off of men of Israel's tradition with no future on railroad ramp,
all this meant Baden-Baden had joined the blood-bath pool of the anti-Semite camp.

on the night and terror of *Kristallnacht* – when human decency was for naught,
there was cruelty engineered and manufactured propaganda thought;
this *aktion* the Nazis poisoned literature inflamed, until hateful people willed and sought,
was what headmaster Leo Wohleb at the *gymnasium* courageously fought.

Greek and Latin dramas were taught at *Hohenbaden* instead of rigid state indoctrination,
as the academic standard for *Juden* and gentile *abitur* education;
admission, prizes, awards for Jewish students embattled without justification;
until all Baden-Baden *Juden* were removed, murdered— one stone for absolution.

James R. Ellerston
November 18, 2013

J.F.K.— Once On Those Days Fifty Years Ago

I have a memory hidden deep down
in a part of me I don't visit very often;
I held a dream inside tucked somewhere
in the back of my internal closet
from a dynamic President's speech when I was eleven,
until "one giant step for all mankind" when I had turned nineteen,
and a young man's vision became a historic lunar truth.

I have a memory of days at home in 1963,
wrapped in a blanket against the November chills
on a day home from junior high school;
I watched the long parade
and saw the child salute;
The slow horse drawn wheels rolled on the street;
The loss was beat into my mind
with the cadence of the drums;
We are a generation that remembers
where we were that day and heard the news
with snowy visions of black and white television
in school cafeterias of shattered national innocence;
The school secretary had handed a note to our beloved music teacher,
smile wiped from his ex-Navy whitened face,
our band breathless, silenced;
Airless horns lay unimportant in sickened laps until dismissal,
our ears tuned only to the scratch of an early transistor radio—
hearing the pain that has endured since.

He made footprints moving our nation with the joy of youth,
and I have watched the televised moon pictures again and again
through the window of adolescent dream and loss.

James R. Ellerston
November 20, 2013

A High Price to Pay (Rittenhouse Market on Spruce Street)

on an overcast day in Philadelphia, chilly,
in a small central-city grocery
the kind with pails of fresh flowers in front
for would-be young lovers,
and higher prices on the shelves
for smaller-sized cans than would feed a family—
but ideal for the single person
or the diminished appetite of the aging,
searching for satisfaction for an isolated tongue
that doesn't taste any longer with enthusiasm.

she pushed the cart up to the cashier
followed by shuffling steps trailing behind
made by aged legs in rubber goulashes over leather shoes;
her stubborn weariness lifted the diminutive cans upon the counter—
the efficient check-out scheme in slow-motion now
as the few items were precisely placed in a row
like treasured items for a pawn-broker's pittance.

the elderly woman stood there apart, distracted,
handing over bills reverently one after another,
watching items disappearing into a filmy plastic sack,
taking the bag and moving urgently away in wobbling steps—
the cashier following hastily after
pressing paper change into blue-veined arthritic fingers, daily,
with calmness and gentleness
questioning once again "Are you alright today?"

the woman in light-headed confusion
tottered an isolated moment, nodding,
responding to the unexpected kindness, received
as she was checking-out habitually from daily life;
her gloveless hands braced for a few familiar blocks
in rubber boots on a dampened cold street—
the wind whipping thin gray strands as the auto-door opened harshly,
to the quickened world outside
unto the path of her solitary steam-heated three-flights-up rooms.

such is the price of growing old alone
in brave solitude
in central-city Philadelphia
without a relative to make your old-age home.

James R. Ellerston
November 30, 2013

Burial of Veteran Gower

In fields outside the town of Lohrville,
      found on detailed Iowa highway maps,
Amid harvested corn and under swaying pines
      upon a grassy stone pocked hill,
His life's moments ended upon this lonely knoll
      with his gathered family hearing bugle taps;
He had fought disease for struggling days
      moving closer to death with stubborn will,
And was laid to rest near his hometown friends,
      partly a soldier still.

Rifles fired rounds—their sharp cracks bit the winds,
      casings picked up somberly from the fertile ground,
The hearse speedily brought an honored Illinois coffin
      on a stately black Cadillac ride,
There was snap of fabric and folded flag
      softly presented the daughter with grateful sound;
Young soldiers and small-town Legionnaires
      did their duties confidently in stride,
And mounting the bronze plaque upon his stone
      will proclaim him a veteran with God as his guide.

Two young soldiers in military dress
      stood at coffin's foot and head,
From Fort Des Moines they traveled far
      to fold the flag and honor him,
The bugler stood firm and intoned his tune—
      those standing listened with hearts of lead;
He has passed from earthly life now,
      his vision sudden turned dim,
But memories remain of youthful days of service,
      "the greatest generation" more than passing whim.

His daughter and friends stood quietly posed
        around newly dug brazen black earth;
He was called up dutifully during World War Two,
        and sailed across an ocean to fight the bitter strife;
He waited patiently for daughter's loving marriage
        and two grandchildren at their birth;
Surviving war he came home a stronger seasoned man,
        ever tender-true to his school-marm love and life-long sweet-heart wife,
An adult child he always cherished now mourned in chill autumn air,
        one who kindly cared gently for him during a long parental life.

The report of six guns saluting cracked abruptly on the hill,
        cutting cool breezes wafting country peaceful air,
Combines and laden wagons paraded by raising clouds,
        silence at the stately gravesite to them made human sense,
A sunny day for roaring harvesters, quiet burial, honor, grief—
        the release of final death—his end of earthly care;
The lone daughter, young spouse, and grandchildren stood
        like soldiers at stiff attention (so quiet, rigid, tense),
Remembering a father missing at supper's table,
        an empty chair for tomorrows hence.

Formal memorial services are held in cities,
        with organ hymn-bursts in churches of stone,
'Cause the truth is that old soldiers do age in life,
        succumb to ravaging illness and therefore die,
Despite seamless military services finding no grieving veteran's family
        feeling unprotected at death's confronting door alone;
With such beloved now sudden gone, and those distant held closer dear,
        one relies on faith's strong heal, to weep dry tears and still convulsive cry,
As life's slow vehicles move down graveled roads found rocky,
        dust rolling in progress toward distant heaven's sky.

James R. Ellerston
Nov. 4-7, 2013

"Imagine" a Christmas in 1913
(Singer with piano plays "Imagine" before riot police in Kiev: Dec. 8, 2013)

imagine a scene on the world stage—
painted as the last Christmas with values of the 19th century
when world order was still comfortable
and families in small cottages and the great houses
could still live and die with predictability;
German, Russian, French, and British sons
who grew up on the land
would probably stay on the land;
shepherds herded their sheep and tilled wheat
not only in carols but on actual cold moonlit nights,
when stars shown bright in the hilly fields of familial ancestors;
"no hell below us,
above us only sky..."

the dead were still laid to rest in individual graves
in family plots of stone and wrought iron
after lives led by the still waters and green pastures,
and only a few miles from home on farms
or ethnic city neighborhoods where families
of immigrants from the same country spoke the same language
and eked out meager incomes in bitter factories
owned by stockholders and the captains of industry;
but all held one day reserved to rest the same,
sang similar carols in their native tongues
while most of the planet was still at a real peace;
"imagine, a brotherhood of man,
sharing all the world..."

the Eve night was silent except the joy of hopeful music;
great choirs and organs praised the "Prince of Peace"
while European empires built their giant iron dreadnoughts
amid only shadows formed before the summers embattled conflict
fired the machines and mechanized guns of seventeen nations
and entrenched young men in years of hellish attrition,
ending in a stalemate which didn't end all wars;
"imagine there's no countries...
it isn't hard to do..."

imagine a scene on the world stage—
by the next year those who volunteered or were conscripted manhood
became mourned as empty chairs from the shell-hole burial plots
of a generation soon to be lost as fodder;
in a year lighted candles would honor those away
eating their rations,
reading the same scriptures,
keeping their heads below the parapet
with only moments left in their young life to imagine;
"nothing to kill or die for...
living life in peace..."

imagine a scene on the world stage—
bad treaties and mixed ethnic borders created new political nations
after the global warfare ended forever
hopes of peace in all earth's lands—
the times when once every son had come back from feeding stabled stock
with hay-filled mangers before the night became colder, darker;
all ages sitting at the Christmas Eve table near home fires burning
blessing family life and food and hearth's warm flame
according to the old world's notions of farming seasons;
"you may say I'm a dreamer
but I'm not the only one..."

imagine a scene on the world stage—
a photo was taken after bravely
a man pushed a blue and yellow piano into the street in Kiev—
onto an Independence Square filled with riot police with shields;
the solitary man sat down and sang the lyrics of a universal song
written by an artist gunned down, his body martyred, killed;
John Lennon's words flowed out over a city's freedom struggle
in clear solo tenor to a Ukraine locked in protest;
"imagine all the people
sharing all the world..."

James R. Ellerston
December 11, 2013
excerpts from "Imagine" by John Lennon
for the Encore Singers of Iowa Central Community College
Kathleen Schreier, director
performances on December 12, 13, 2013

a mere royal pardon for Alan

a name known at universities but not in common knowledge,

Turing put food on war-torn British tables;

a flotilla of ships floated on his formulated mathematical sea;

the great docks of Liverpool unloaded algorithms

spinning at Bletchley on his calculators solving codes;

before him great WW2 convoys sailed supply lines

while Nazi wolf-packs directed by Enigma picked them off

with U-boat superiority sending them to the bottom of the North Atlantic;

by his genius a nation didn't starve on limited calories;

he broke the codes— the Axis;

thousands of Allied soldiers and sailors lived in a shorter war

due to his breaking the secret of the enemies' communications.

his futuristic advances in computing were held secret for fifty years—

innovative mechanical machines were destroyed in fear,

keeping them from the Cold War Soviets.

he was labeled a criminal by a homo-phobic culture

which crucified him with injected female hormones,

destroying his agile body and generous mind,

now sterilized by chemicals by those of lesser imagination.

his death by accident or suicide remains a question,

but his genius so hampered was gone for sure;

an apple by a bedside let cyanide do its work.

continued

an antique Queen on the Eve of Christmas pardoned

his singular offense after decades,

but failed in limits of royal mercy

by not freeing from court-imposed sentences

another similarly convicted fifty-thousand,

guilty of no crime against humanity;

fifty-thousand who faced stigma for no decreed sin

but being true to their own normality;

this bigotry by previous courts still upheld—

untold wasted genius left to languish.

the Queen could only do a parade-wave

at just this world-celebrated one—

such a slight ineffective gesture

when so much good could have been done.

James R. Ellerston

January 1, 2014

boots still wearing black shirts beating black hats

they ran from us and we chased them down,
falling, bleeding, muttering prayers,
sheltering their skulls with bruised hands—
weak men unwilling to fight back in the world,
unwilling to serve in our noble military cause.

they are our designated scum
and will not wage the weapons of war for our land,
they will not make our nation triumphant,
superior over our neighbors.
we will bring them into line, encamp them, train them.

I trim my scalp close, daily shave my face,
(no beards like them, no long hair
drawn back in Samson weakness);
I proudly wear my uniforms of youthful power,
my black-shirted uniform, (no white collar of purity for us).

even in the desert land, I wear no hat like them;
my short hair signifies present authority and past horrors;
I beat them with my police baton or truncheon,
knocking-off their hats of ancient costume,
un-robing survivors that migrated here from other nations.

these black wide-brimmed hats were worn by men
who also hoped to call this nation their home
(our nation of armed force feared for our warfare,
and developer of exotic atomic weaponry)
we have scientists; they refuse to serve in our military.

their scholars would prefer to sit in Jewish seminaries and study,
and expect the nation to provide for their academic lives—
but their holy life is useless to our military nation;
we will not accept their stubborn lives;
I beat them, chase them along hard stone walls.

As a black-shirted Nazi I did this for the Reich,
and saw them imprisoned, their pride of million's killed;
I now hunt down my Orthodox Jewish neighbors in crowds
because I am an Israeli policemen or government soldier
and they protest the nation's laws including all in service.

I beat their kind because they will not be an imprisoned killer
and murder their neighbors who they do not understand
upholding miles of barbed-wire, concrete walls, and gates
for a line in the sand at a desert border crossing
or West Bank *lebensraum* we arm and settle.

for our walled-in defensive camp hit by outside rockets
we now claim a God-given right to fire rockets back,
this ragged portion of the lands of Palestine we bought with Jewish blood;
now it is the Orthodox Jew who still walks among us,
toward taught hardened hatred I swing my law-given brutal club.

who now is the current parasite on the ancient tribes of Israel
among survivors of the Diaspora and the Holocaust traveling together?
the crime is as old as the upheld ancient scrolls,
and again does not make the western TV evening news
across a still anti-Semite globe, still not covering heads in shame.

James R. Ellerston
February 7, 2014

Standing with You, Ukraine

stomping cold feet in the dirty snowy street;

we gather around barrels of searing flame behind barricades;

a man chops wood, splitting it for warmth;

another carries a black tire over his sagging shoulder;

cold winds blow as snow swirls in icy drifts;

comrades pile tires and timbers higher across an intersection;

holding sheltering government buildings gives us a rotation from the storm

lines of state police in riot gear in defensive order corralling us;

men and women in our ranks have stood firm almost two united months;

Orthodox priests have come and blessed the peacefulness of our cause

standing firm for a nation once again hopeful of democratic sovereignty;

expensive natural gas flows through the essential bowels

of urban industrialized life in the gray blight of rows of bloc apartments;

Caucasus wells hold a people's future hostage for pipeline prices and sovereign debt;

yes, regional differences within borders divide us based on language and geography;

some in our country fear yearn-full eyes looking toward European nations;

but funds to be designated by the bright lights of western democracy

may give us a chance to negotiate for a better life in partnership

free of an infectious imprisonment with the totalitarian Bear

whose stench of gaseous fumes flows beneath the very streets we occupy—

if ever so briefly for hope of life in freedom.

James R. Ellerston

February 4, 2014

choosing responsibility vs. morality

pain today to have tomorrow;
rights of a parent,
rights of a child;
two years earlier than Netherlands twelve years
of age to make a decision;
giving life hope,
having no life hope;
a legal age at which to decide to die,
a legal age at which to decide to kill;
to die by withholding medicine,
to die by giving assistance;
a parent's agony,
a child's wish;
removing a patient's pain,
merely pulling the plug,
switching off the machines;
a doctor's ethics,
(a Nazi history)
a nation's morality;
child euthanasia in Belgium 2014,
a tenth birthday present of deadly choice;
but few children
with a kind nurse
or feeling parental love would choose
not to have a goodnight kiss,
a tomorrow night of wondrous stars,
and to have the story read to them again.

James R. Ellerston
February 15, 2014

really hearing the shoes on the street

they thought they were condemned
until a Swiss flag flew over their safe-house;
but in the night the ugly came
the Arrow-Cross, young Hungarian fascist thugs
came in terror for other Hungarians (Jews);
they were forcibly marched to the River Danube
stood passive along its flowing shore;
heard orders gruffly barked to line up your shoes
(to leave them on the embankment in pairs)
lose all modesty by removing sheltering clothes;
cold cruelty stepped along their line behind them,
Oh, to be next in the nightmare—
they waited for the bullet to enter their brain;
bodies fell into the surging water, into the dark—
names gone from modern memory,
shoes left on death's divide.

these now gone except for sixty pairs of memorial shoes
cast in iron by the sculptor Gyula Pauer,
molded in styles they wore some seven decades ago—
men's, women's, and children's shoes and boots
that were so hastily removed,
their owners bare skin feeling the coldness
of embittered young men's lack of soul,
as next to them bodies toppled into the swirling water,
swept away from the embankment in wartime currents;
but now memorialized by sixty pairs of iron shoes,
as if waiting for the owners' strolling return along the promenade.
while anti-Semitism rears its ugly head again,
in a modern Hungary trying to redeem itself
with even another new Holocaust museum being built
in an appeal for absolution from its hateful past;

today gangs of black-shirted young toughs
cruelly roam historically already-pained streets;
but tourists are the ones made to feel the heartache
by the sixty pairs of cast iron shoes
when they come to see the famous Iron Bridge
connecting Buda and Pest
in the background of a story where past hatred lives on;
well shod are the stinking feet of those who take a militant stride
to persecute Hungarian Jewry today;
iron hearts still goose-stepping to a persecuting tune,
iron heels on stairs before other knocks on doors.

James R. Ellerston
February 18, 2014

on February 18th, 2014

what is your story youthful teen boy of Kiev
as you walk by the hulk of a truck on fire,
legs wrapped to prevent blows,
head sheltered by helmet sturdy and orange,
hands gloved against bitter cold,
back, chest, thighs protected by homemade shields?

your face gazes stern into the photographer's lens;
Reuters has done their sober job again;
no smile masks the determination in your eyes;
what is that you carry in your hand?
(sweets or biscuits for a child?)
you walk on through the fighting toward the barricades.

all of fourteen years of age, but
focused, dedicated, feeling your young manhood,
caught up in the circumstances of your life
you are on your way to a harsh short schooling,
to be educated in the art of urban warfare
where conviction turns a boy into a freedom fighter.

twenty-six have died today, scores already are wounded
by sticks, stones, real bullets and flaming Molotov cocktails;
blessed first-aid is given inside the golden-domed cathedral;
will you survive your baptism by fire?
(I stare at the color photo which will remain of this time
and may forever memorialize your innocent life.)

James R. Ellerston
February 19, 2014

beatitudes for Kiev *Maidan*

blessed be the carriers of tires and stones in heavy bags, for they
    reinforced the square to be defended;

blessed be those who manned the walls, for they
    turned piles of timber and rubber into the burning strength of men's hearts;

blessed are the breakers of paving stones, for these hopeful righteous
    made pieces to throw at those who did not keep their distance;

blessed by those who mourn fallen earthly lives, for the newly dead
    shall be long honored in their country's history;

blessed be those who administered medicine in hospital and out, for they
    worked in the street, church, and hotel lobby to save the wounded;

blessed be those who fight foreign aggression,
    for the world knows them as patriots;

blessed be the parents who weep for a dead child,
    for their offspring gave all to a dedicated cause;

blessed be those who defend constitutional law, for they
    shall oust the despots who would oppress;

blessed be the negotiators who work long hours in the name of justice,
    to convince both sides of the possibilities of a better future;

blessed be the calming priests and choirs that sang of God, for they
    reminded the multitudes of something larger overlooking their struggles;

blessed be the builders of defensive barricades, for their battles they
    shall inherit the freedoms of democratic lives.

James R. Ellerston
February 21, 2014

Catherine Ashton came from Brussels

she came to Independence Square, and brought
the hope of bundled yellow tulip blooms
wrapped in a new cellophane political transparency
laid down for all the world to see, in recognition
by a union of nations now mourning the dead of another,
and together with weeping individuals offered flowers
carefully placed on stacked tires and bricks at the *Maidan,*
now a memorial open again letting in streams of people,
carrying the cross of a nation in common purpose,
rivers of flowing tears.

in the peaceful quiet of Kiev's city square once in such turmoil
uniformed policemen now kneel before relieved citizens
asking forgiveness for crimes against their nation;
a people are open to those seeking repentance, now mourning,
with plans to prosecute the makers of poor decisions—
those who ordered the gunfire at the barricades
cascading innocent deaths with no absolution, but today
the hope of bundled yellow tulip blooms
wrapped in a new cellophane political transparency
is laid down for all the world to see, on camera,
for all to grieve with cheers.

James R. Ellerston
February 25, 2014

Société Nationale des Chemins de fer Francais (SNCF)

this question of ethics, morality, and corporate responsibility
involves bids on certain American commuter train lines
amid this diverse nation of justice owning states,
first in California and now in Maryland by *Keolis*, a subsidiary.

compensation requirements were vetoed in California
and negotiations with the French government
are now underway when Maryland's light-rail bids
by the French owned subsidiary came under fire.

the question is one of legal responsibility to those who moved to America,
and the corporation as an extent person whose life lives on;
should it be historically responsible for its previous actions?
(even the American subsidiary of the French parent company?)

the contested company is owned by the current French government;
yet a previous French government had signed an armistice with the Nazis,
placed itself and its trains into the Nazis' service, locked the cattle-car doors,
and hauled people from their hellish confinement at places like *Drancy*.

they hauled 76,000 on one-way trips to final destinations in death camps;
debaters claim there is no *tort* law to be enforced on those who cooperated
because the riders didn't purchase tickets on the French trains
for their standing ride in jammed cattle cars (11,000 children).

the riders had no expectations for the purchase of any return tickets
to be sold to homeward bound riders either, only two thousand made it back;
most paid dearly for their transport in a tortured era
when "return by air" meant drifting clouds of rising crematorium smoke.

James R. Ellerston
February 26, 2014

nursing civil war in the Crimean Peninsula

there will be no Florence Nightingale
with her band of nurses
sailing to the Crimea this time,
or the dedicated others like her:
Mary Seacole, of mixed race like mingled Crimean populace,
or Mother Francis Bridgeman, with her aseptic clinics,
who came to save the warriors from their diseased selves,
so they would live to see home again.

there will be no one diplomat alone
making sterile rounds with a lamp of truth
held at midnight deadline with a treaty in germ free hand
coming to save these men's lives
from the horrors of undeclared ethnic war
as nationalities again fight the rampant diseases
of possessiveness and control
over this small peninsula.

this is a place where the ethnicity of different lingual races
becomes something to battle over in the streets,
in a world of contagious political disease,
and photographed wounded civil warriors,
emblazoned across front pages to justify politics
embattled to see whose Parliament shall have control—
who shall have the final word of sovereignty?
and who shall fight for union with old or new empires?

this is a chasm where the behaviors of warfare
are fought over past naval station treaties
and entrenched claims to an international sea
however Black with the dried blood
of historical centuries of dead and wounded
no matter how well nursed and hospitalized,
no matter whose ships now freely sail
through the Bosporus of a democratic land,
to a Crimea under the international lens
and threatening diplomatic pens.

James R. Ellerston
February 27, 2014

Half-Rhymes Ramping Up

Ukraine is sovereign
but military jets create tension
as army maneuvers threaten moving in
supposedly to protect ethnic brethren kin;
a battle for Crimea is justified by Vladimir Putin
because of diplomacy by those EU who are foreign,
those not understanding naval needs distinctly Russian.

James R. Ellerston
February 27, 2014

fußball is universal

the boy within kicks a *fußball*,
outside in truth is a young man in Ukrainian uniform
part of a brave army to protect the national people,
but so far in Crimea his guns haven't fired a shot—
no bullets have broken the tension of the generals' game.

the serviceman kicks a *fußball*
in this semi-autonomous geographical region of the field,
where armored personnel carriers lining roads
have brought in a foreign army with Russian aims,
but with no insignia on their team uniforms

the man kicks a *fußball*
on the grassy field of cold confrontation
encumbered by the weight of his soldiers fatigues,
and the backdrop of opposing military vehicles,
at the *Belbek* airport in Crimea.

the soldier kicks a *fußball*
while awaiting the words that will save his nation
after the requests of an exiled President—
from a foreign military intervention
into his region of ethnicity and confrontation.

a peacemaker kicks a *fußball*
toward the goal in the scruffy winter's grass,
a spot held steadfast in the minds of all embattled—
going home to hearth, home, and family;
the young man dreams and kicks again.

there are no referees in this game on Ukraine's home field;
young men play at war on opposing sides of iron gates of hatred;
but unlike the Christmas Truce of 1914 on the Western Front
they have not used their armaments before this day in a no-mans-land,
and would rather score by living together united to see another game.

James R. Ellerston
March 4, 2014

Taras Shevchenko at Two Hundred Years

your forty-seven years,
celebrated again this March 9th, 2014,
saw only a day of living after that last birthday party;
your death as a freed serf
came just seven days before
the Emancipation Reform of 1861
proclaimed the liberty
of more than twenty-three million people,
(including your own siblings),
freed people who gained the right to own property,
to own a business,
or to buy land from a landlord. (your dream).
as a serf artist and poet you were duty bound
to the land where you were born,
and expected to make payments to your landlord—
but you wrote poetry of such expressive beauty
that your freedom was bought for you
by others of artistic sensitivity;
(funds were raised by the donation and lottery
sale of a portrait which freed you on May 5, 1836).

a life of travel and exile
caused your heart to ache
for your beloved Ukraine—
and as you inspired your countrymen
with the soul of nationalism,
your writing formed the foundation
for modern Ukrainian literature;
you are often credited as the founder
of the modern written Ukrainian language;
your painted pictures, drawings, etchings impacted
the lives of others with your unique artistic talent;
though schooled in classic painting techniques,
you were ready to experiment—
especially with the new photographic art.

your remains after initial burial, were moved
with honor to be buried in the soil of Ukraine
as you had expressed in your "*Testament*";
"Oh bury me, then rise ye up and break your heavy chains";
a grave now marked by covered mound in tranquil field;
there are imposing monuments to your poetry
across the globe in distant major cities
erected by the Ukrainian *diaspora*;
these remind today's Ukrainians
that the greatest of their own nation
have had difficult lives fighting on a personal level
for a life of freedom of expression,
not bound in shackles of serfdom, servitude, slavery,
or Russian territorial ambitions.

James R. Ellerston   March 9, 2014   Recognitions on the 200th anniversary of his birth (1814-1861)

Ghosts of Mile 59

I left behind my home in Ireland in 1832;
we came from the Ulster Counties of *Donagal*, *Tyrone*, and *Dern*;
I was hired on as one of a team of fifty-seven men;
but my American dream was shorter than two months then.

A world-wide cholera pandemic swept us through,
along the railroad's Pennsylvania wooded, shaded grade
my friends and I once buried together in a ditch
near Malvern in hidden glade as dark as pitch.

Now Amtrak trains roll on electrified in sunshine;
where the secrets of my group's demise lay filed, dormant
hidden, suppressed until one hundred sixty years had passed
through the work we done for Phillip Duffy, money was amassed.

Our work is known as Duffy's Cut by people living now
they denied us in dire illness the needed medicinal care;
our lives before were prejudiced against us, as Irish Catholics we say;
we passed away as immigrant workers, expendable in progress' way.

Immaculata historians first found some bones in the year 2009,
more research at our miserable site suggested a mass murder
'cause the first two located skulls suggested a purposeful deadly drama;
by vigilantes fearful and panicked our cholera would spread its trauma.

Analysis of my brother workers' bones tells of possible fired guns;
a short life of muscular work with long-term impoverished sickness
a story of life in a derelict Shantytown, in fear of germs burned down;
we made a rail bed still in use, moved dirt mountains around Malvern town.

With our backs we labored to our deaths to fill in that ravine
mine was the sixth body recovered there, recovered bones now seen,
our toil became our burial site, long hidden near busy rails;
and I'm the only one named John Ruddy, in history's forgotten tales.

no money for DNA was found, so expensive is its worth.
so no analysis of expensive DNA has yet to prove my birth;
I miss a molar in my jaw like my Irish-descended clan;
this is a rare thing found once in a million in a single Irish man.

They thought I came from *Inishowen* in County *Donegal*,
some of the other remains are now enshrined in Pennsylvania at Bala Cynwyd;
but my worker brothers won't see Ireland's shore again;
others are still buried beneath steel commuter tracks around the bend.

My bones dug up, were one day packed in a bed of Bubble Wrap.
my packed bones boxed and carried, and shipped UPS from Philly
with a care beyond what's normal for such old fragile things,
to a ceremony of final rest and honor, with a truth that soulfully rings.

My remains soared flying across the wide Atlantic again,
sailing above the sea where earlier the *John Stamp* had rolled;
I once was an eager lad of only eighteen looking westward on that deck,
the youngest in my hired-on railroad gang, whose final mystery they did check.

We are now honored by movies and a National Opera premiere
and remains buried with the soil of our native land;
my own bones and all of me under a monument to forever stand,
have been interned in a town in *Donegal,* in Ireland.

I was somehow finally buried near to my dear hometown *Inishowen*
in my misty green and emerald but poor Irish shores,
with a ceremony accompanied by a priest, three pipers clad in kilts;
Irish sentiment not discarded in death, like a bouquet of flowers wilts.

James R. Ellerston
March 10-11, 2014

Dead Child of a Nation's Hope (March 11, 2014)

His mother awakened him like every early morn'
soon her beloved healthy youngest from her, wounded was torn;
age fourteen he went out early for the fresh-baked daily bread
his head was hit and fatally damaged, injured instead.

In his Turkish *Alevi* culture bread is held as somewhat blessed,
if dropped, is touched to lips and kissed, then to the forehead pressed;
the family's youngest to fetch the breakfast daily is so honored;
his last trip by gun-fired tear gas canister was deadly marred.

A protesting nation hoping for healing counted each infected day
over 269 sunsets to thirty-five pounds he shrank, as in hospital he lay;
at age fifteen he finally succumbed one tearful morning gray,
in minds of marching protestors, "Immortal" their chanting began to say.

Bread tied with black ribbons set out on doorsteps, and candles bitterly lit,
unfortunately his coffin's parade won't help calls for democracy one bit;
Berkin Elvan was a child full of parents' hope and nation's love,
who didn't get their young boy's life extended by Allah above.

James R. Ellerston
March 13, 2014

Agent Orange Orphans Debased in Vietnam

My ancestors lived when you fought your brutal war here,
invading our country with deadly force and fire,
but it was the insidious nature of the Monsanto defoliant
sprayed over the jungles that changed my life.

Now I am an orphan of parental rejection
of my genetically altered human form,
birth defects so irreconcilable to my mother
that I now spend my days in an orphanage.

We are the wards of the charity of others' kind labor
to keep us clean each day, fed, and bathed;
we live out our lives in a sterile white room,
spending days in stainless steel cages, no parent's love have we.

Our grandparents were left behind in the jungle and cities
and when the last 'copter left the embassy roof in Saigon;
these babies-not-killed remained in the country and survived to adulthood,
but later as parents were not ready for our ever frequently deformed occurrence.

The ugliness is that you lost not only the war but left us a generation behind,
our devastated parents and rooms full of warehoused orphans, will grow up
hating you for what rained down from your righteous 'star-spangled' sky,
and reluctance to pay compensation to help orange-clouded lives in Vietnam.

James R. Ellerston
March 17, 2014

hole in the truth

morning
security fence
Palestinian youths
age 12 and 15
suspected sabotage
call to surrender
Israeli soldier
warning shots
main suspect
wounded
medical team
hospital
death
age 15
picking thistle
hole in barrier
stones thrown
wounded
martyr
resistance
get income
anger
racism
cold blooded aim
stones thrown
tear gas
power
arrested
other 12 year old friend
afternoon
funeral
parade
village
international news
truth?
perspective?

angels in a hot zone

trying to avoid touching the outside air
is the goal for children of the Fukushima cataclysm
some of whom have almost never played outdoors
and stayed indoors, and try to stay healthy,
no longer young and innocent—
when you must change out of protective clothes
worn on a normal thirty minute kindergarten recess
and change to indoor garments free of contamination
in order to play in an indoor sand pit—
clothes changing easing the fears of worried parents,
living with straining or strengthening family bonds.

children now weigh more
have the possibility of the development of thyroid cancer,
and show a drop in physical strength,
both apparent in indoor athletic competitions;
video games are a salvation for indoor captivity
when going out or opening the window are now forbidden
for those in a sheltering annex hidden from the nuclear poison
these young internal refugees hide—
hide from a life changing Gestapo of radioactivity,
(an enemy silent, ruthless, deadly, but measurable)
from which there is no amnesty
but only shelter from the invisible heat
and the armistice in this battle
is called a half-life
(of atomic particles or one's family)
and a clean-up war expected to last forty years,
half a normal lifetime for those who will be grandparents
and today can only dream of unaffected grandchildren
while debates of nuclear safety go on
and windows planned to not be opened are sealed worldwide.

James R. Ellerston March 29, 2014 (credits to Toru Hanai, Reuters)

straw vote

she crosses the field to cast a vote—
this cluttered meadow of straw and grain,
grasses growing the stuff of bread
born up from the ground.

her skirt swings gracefully
through a path of seed and chaff
under the hot mid-day sun,
to the place she will mark her lot.

she crosses the sea of ripened plants
with her innocent child in her hands—
held gracefully or led along beside,
on her roadway through the golden crop.

it has been a long distance
for a women to get to make her choice,
and enter a political world with a child—
hopes for life drives each step across the field.

James R. Ellerston
April 22, 2014

in front of the gun

we worked all day on little food,
cold in thin clothes,
feet rag wrapped, often in snow;
threats of immediate death
for the slightest clumsiness or slowdown;
grieving for lost family members
the unknown and dead tearing at our hearts;
the pain in our heads blocking our starving hurting stomachs.

but now they may extend our pension rights—
more guilt money for our labor in the thousand ghettos
where we were the lucky ones who survived
the slaughter of the six million;
we, the 130,000 former ghetto workers still alive,
now living a dream in modern Israel,
may receive an extra so generous $20,400 dollars
in new pension rights from the present German government
if and when the proposed legislation passes.

we could now claim pension rights back to the year 1997
(a mere 55 years after the wrongs were committed);
remember our own Jewish councils and ghetto police
were forced to enforce the Nazi orders and who should work;
the new December 2013 German government
has pledged to find a solution
to the issue as quickly as possible;
"the check is in the mail" does not make up for the loss
of my mother, father, sister, and brother;
and carrying bricks for the Reich
as a child struggling to put one foot in front of another
and not to fall or stumble in front of the gun.

James R. Ellerston
February 12, 2014

the tap still drips hope

the tap still drips for the Palestinian people;
their children are thirsty,
their children need bathing;
their children are hungry;
the food in their gardens has dried-up;
the wells in villages have gone dry;
the river is being diverted,
it no longer irrigates fields and keeps them green;
cisterns have been smashed,
and now leak bloodshed upon angry youth.

one can build walls to keep peoples apart,
one can buy weapons of war,
one can demolish property,
one can move generations of people;
but to control an area's development
one must be in control of the water;
(an old American Western about the farmer's fence
and the watering-hole for cattle will tell you that).

there will be no peace in the desert
without equal allocation of the water;
without theft of water resources
through massive pipelines from occupied territories;
without stealing away the tourist economies of shore-lands;
without destruction of irrigated agriculture,
villages source of life nourishment.

while one occupying power
controls the rationing of health-giving water
of those who are now occupied,
there will be no long-term peace possible
under international law—
which forbids the stealing of resources
as a reward of warfare and occupation;
the subjugated Palestinians will always thirst
for the wells of freedom in their increasingly dry land.

the hard-driven rains of justice
fall toward embattled Palestinian lives.
a metaphor for cleansing their land of occupiers;
now Israeli occupiers were criticized in the German language
in their own Jewish Knesset
for denying water equality to Palestinians;
this was criticism from a German nation
giving Israel three more submarines
(with which to fight their wars
of mid-east Mediterranean power);
this was criticism by a nation
guilty of proclaiming a thousand year Reich;
this was criticism by a nation
planning to extend German pensions to slave-laborers
who survived in a thousand hateful ghettos
where the water-shortages were also contrived,
and controlled by those who saw themselves as masters.

the hard-driven rains of justice
lash at these windows in time that peace-talks provide;
the tap still drips hope.

James R. Ellerston
February 14, 2014

upright piano takes the world stage

riot police stand in hostile rows with shields
while the carcass of the blue and yellow painted piano
is moved into the focus of the temporary stage again;
a microphone is hurriedly set up,
it howls its tests through mild winter air;
young pianists gather to wait their turn,
dressed warmly without gloves to perform;
a curious audience gathers from behind the barricades;
well-practiced fingers float over familiar keys—
years of home-rehearsed art
at the service of the city's protestors;
nerves are calmed with musical moments;
(temporarily pianistic technique triumphs over confrontation)
giving negotiators yet another day
to discuss the complex future of the nation,
while musical talent triumphs over bloodied brutality,
keeping today peaceful in the city centre of Kiev;
hope is the key they play in—
this Ukrainian rhapsody of emotion.

James R. Ellerston
February 11, 2014

Sitter in Bambari

Find a quiet hour of peace,
       sitting in a doorway with a smile,
a gaze into another's loving eyes
       while breathing the fresh morning air;
plants and flowers growing at one's feet
       springing from the dry soil.

century-old pink plaster
       shelters from the sunlight's rays;
the smell of food
       whispers flavors out a partially opened door,
and hope for life
       emerges with each drawn inhalation.

you sit at her trusted feet
       desiring a closeness that feels like family,
and she crouches in her flowered skirt,
       hands folded in grace,
hair drawn up in a white traditional cloth
       ready to work hard in the afternoon sun.

and her flashing teeth
       articulate comforting words
in a mouth that speaks love
       for the child in her moment's care;
and eyes and lips together today
       know not how to say anything else.

James R. Ellerston
June 13, 2014

something beautiful about ice cream and cheese

still hunting for a home-cooked country meal
we drive into Cornell, Wisconsin's streets
and spy a corner eatery aptly called
Dylan's Ice Cream and Cheese.

a long refrigerated showcase displays cheddars,
multiple kinds of different ages fill the shelf
next to white cheeses with fruits and peppers;
the freezer case displays twenty kinds of homemade ice cream.

on the wall you see Dylan in photos at seventeen years and with leukemia,
and stories that tell of his homegrown wish for "Make A Wish";
it was for a dairy herd to milk morning and night—
for that the Foundation gave him just the first two cows.

town's people donated and held bake sales and raffles;
the herd numbered thirty then later sixty cows;
an old barn unused for twenty years was eagerly prepared;
milk sold to a dairy was bought back, made into floats, cones, and shakes.

his mother opened the small town's corner restaurant in Dylan's name;
the half-pound burger with cheese and a shake
cooked among home-sewn aprons and humorous signs,
spreads a wall-story and bald-headed photo displayed with empathetic fame.

James R. Ellerston
July 27, 2014

leaving home for the front line August 31st

leaving home for the front line August thirty-first;
it is but a Reuters' photo snap in 2014,
a Kurdish instant;
the woman's face is masterfully hidden—
we do not know
if she is filled with agony or pride—
that mixture in every mother's heart
as their 'sun' goes off to the clouds of war.

we see her right arm and wrist bent,
back of hand cradled gracefully against his face
brushing a beard or feeling the stubble of a hasty shave;
we see a left arm and open palm extended downward,
in helpless despondency and surrender to the event,
not reaching up in a hug, opening wells of emotion—
not holding him back one last time,
before her son is forced to become a man.

the photograph is in color
but shows no ashen-faced fears;
his face is masterfully turned aside and hidden;
the boy is bent over from the waist,
light rifle slung across his back;
before her bare feet under her black dress (already mourning)
he stands in white and gray stocking-feet,
like any American kid shoeless wearing Hanes socks on carpet.

unlike an American kid he kisses the back of his mother's hand,
ear-buds blare away the possibility of choking tears;
backpack and water-bottle sit on the floor behind him
betraying his urgency and readiness;
he has volunteered in the Kurdish *peshmerga* forces;
he prepares to leave home for the front line;
he will join forces near *Tuzkhurmatu*;
fighting northeast of *Tikrit* city in Iraq.

his innocent stocking-feet will tramp the boots
of oil-financed warfare;
he wears a black and white scarf around his neck;
his people still have no nation and no flag
(both promised in Cairo in 1923);
the mother says goodbye to her son,
not accepting any finality to their separation;
the boy focuses on the beat of the drummer in his ears.

while his mother speaks so tenderly of sacred love,
sounds of battlegrounds where drummers drown-out pain
play in his teen ears already as real
as any photo-shoot of heart-break can be—
the persons are small in the wide field of white and lavender,
these mere house walls behind defense of home—
he will fight for homeland where the color surrounding his life
will be blood red and men will scream out "mother."

all good in this moment will be blotted out by thundering guns,
yet in a deafened silence he will hear himself in tears—
about today's deadly political world, media, and internet—
where one doesn't dare show their face in a news photo
and knowledgeable foreign journalists know this truth.

James R. Ellerston
September 1, 2014

casualty of the warring world

when you are older we will put a gun in your hand;
we should apologize for doing this to anyone or to you.

now confused, you can hear voices in ringing ears;
you are sitting on the end of a cold doctor's table
like any of us still alive.
any day seeking help from strangers—
those whom you and we trust to "make it better."

unlike any of us, your youthful head is wrapped and bandaged,
your hand and knee are wrapped in gauze;
your blood seeps through sterile cotton,
once white now painfully red;
your eyes swollen shut in hurt purple lines.

your young face shows terror, pain, and shock
about fighting in your neighborhood, your sector,
the rocket blast that hit your apartment house
and the bomb exploded in a crowded market as you fled;
we should apologize for doing this to anyone or to you.

we are fighting for a government, a clan, a religion;
fighting over boundary, border, or fence,
the right to speak or study our native language,
the right of nationhood in our own land for our own people;
all important ideals that warrant a bandage for some.

we fight on for pitiful ideologies
hoping to find a solution for unsolved problems
and creating new open wounds,
over decades old questions, ancient lines on antique maps;
we should apologize for doing this to anyone, or to you.

when you are older we will put a gun in your hand;
we should apologize for doing this to anyone or to you.

James R. Ellerston
September 4, 2014

hatred

throw a rock,
throw a rock with force,
really put your arm into it;

eyes on the target,
head filled with effort,
heart filled with anger;

body bent into the goal,
inflict injury on them—
they whom my elders hate—
whom they talk of at meals
curse and swear after eating,
my grandparents say they are bad;

pick up a rock
put my entire body into it,
stepping forward with hate stinging my eyes
with tears of anguish
for my dead relatives;

look and see no enemy in the bombed out spaces,
while all I have is my rock and arm;
I am too young to be issued a gun
or plant a roadside bomb—
yet I can hate them.

James R. Ellerston
October 17, 2014

Clay Artistry by Palestinian Eyad Sabbah

the young boy:
stares at the child held across the man's chest,
hanging in hope to his shoulder;

the boy experienced:
the anxious anguish of being uprooted
from a home he watched destroyed;

the sculptor's skilled vision:
marriage of eye and hands—
fingers moving wet clay onto a frame
creating a person in motion—
the statues stand on the eve of a new life;
no home in what was once home;

(somehow escaping a bomb blast
in the nick of time):
these persons were later modeled
by an artist of realism—
sculpting terra-cotta for eternity,
and knowing their present story
is today's displacement of battle.

James R. Ellerston
October 21, 2014

guarding the dead's memory (Cpl. Nathan Cirillo)

guarding the National War Memorial,
one might consider a safe duty;
but the cunning mind of the gunman
laid the marching young soldier to the ground—
his family and Canada into mourning;
bagpipes wailing, wreaths laid,
and a wife and child were swept with grief
as the streets and churches wept,
while marching in a solemn parade
from the monument for the unknown lost,
to the bitter stone of one man's burial
in his hometown of Hamilton, Ontario.

Home from the daily struggle

In our world of constant battle, conflict,
of bloodshed, bombs, and terrible disease,
it is the brief union of two lovers,
one tired, tried, at home in daily task surviving inner tension—
one on the field of battle, now home so short a time.

There is the brightest briefest moment of first encounter,
flooded with emotion of blood-veins gushing,
a thrill of beginning and thanksgiving;
known by these who wishfully waited in earnest terror subdued—
for the long-voyage ship entering port with one's own on deck along the rail,
the long-distance bomber that returns from a mission sputtering but with all wheels down,
the National Guard unit returning to the local armory at attention for final salute.

No matter what the deployment or volunteer partisan action,
even the movements of a dark shadowy evening's *résistance*,
it is not for the flag-waving patriots these things happen.
but it is for the returned union of two lovers, gamblers both—
cards and chips that are the perfumed smell of familiar skin, sweat, and leather,
the cushioning hold of gathering arms,
the crushing moment of anguished celebration of return,
eyes closed, sobs and tears of helpless joy;
this love is the only real taste of victory and peace of mind that will last,
firm held in memory beyond the grave of one of those involved.

A person could be at least, at last, be home safe from work a suburban day,
when there is no glow of sunset in the western sky
in a life-threatening mid-western blizzard, with desperate cancellations on the car radio,
one could as well be writing a war-zone news release across the sea,
or fighting a fatal epidemic on the west coast of Africa;
and until the telephone rings, a text, or the internet replies with a flash of hope,
that person dreams of hearing the familiar car in the drive or tread on the stairs—
family dog rushing to the door faster than one can out-run;
the door of time's possibilities swinging and the heart clicking open.

James R. Ellerston
September 16, 2014

To My Son (Kiev, Ukraine October 19, 2014)

I look into your eyes
as you say goodbye to me your mother
and hush your words with the tips of my fingers
on the soft skin of your silenced lips—
no words being adequate for this moment;

You try to comfort my arm gently—
holding it with your massive uniform glove of strength,
betraying the tenderness of your boy's soft skinned hand;

You have taken an oath of allegiance to our country
above all else, family, and lover;

I see a redness in your eyes
and stroke the blond stubble on your shaved face—
a brief comfort, but there is terror—
of losing you in young manhood
as you stand in front of me, as you are now
in this final moment of innocent beauty and youth.

James R. Ellerston
October 23, 2014

imagine a better world (1914-2014)

one hundred years ago this year
"'twas the night before Christmas"
on the Western Front;
the guns on both sides became silent;
and lights appeared over the German lines;
voices joined in chorus,
sonorous sounds drifting across the no man's land
separating the sons of fathers and mothers——
the tired embattled men on both sides.

it began snowing,
obscuring a full moon;
"stille nacht" drifted on the night air;
food was lobbed into opposing trenches,
soldiers applauding each others singing;
Christ trees were erected on the German lines;
"don't shoot, we will send you some bier";
the opposing officers walked out, met, saluted;
the unofficial truth
was that they agreed not to fire on Christmas Day,
to meet and fraternize,
to play soccer between the wires;
the official truth was "a chance to bury the dead",
and read the 23rd psalm over the graves of both sides;
"He makes me lie down in green pastures";
but there was no green grass,
only frozen earth and snow beneath worn boots.

by commanders official orders the guns were not to be silenced again
until the eleventh hour of the eleventh day of the eleventh month,
after the four more years of carnage
which followed that one quiet day of Christmas peace in 1914.

James R. Ellerston
October 30, 2014

They didn't come home after the game (in Ukraine)

Every parent dreads their child not coming home,
when they go out to play with their lads;
kicking the ball with adolescent vigor across the green grass.

They only meant to play a soccer match upon the field,
not on the battlefield it was to become, and scene of death;
the wonderful kick to center field came down, was a "real bomb".

In reality the next play wasn't finished
when the artillery shell landed,
blew its crater in the green grass and stopped the match.

On their school playing field near Donetsk
two of the players died,
and four of my son's friends were wounded on the turf.

They were playing, kicking the ball around for pleasure,
their young bodies sweating with love for the game,
on an otherwise sunny afternoon.

This was a day for fun, to be alive,
before the day grown men wept
and carried my son's white-draped body in a coffin.

James R. Ellerston
November 7, 2014

Joshua Wong (on Your 5th day of Hunger)

We find you in a desert of decision
lacking nourishment of body and spirit;
At eighteen years you have
captured the mind of the world
by becoming a voice on the media
of Scholarism, the hope of young Chinese
of student age fighting the Bejing government
in hopes of a true democracy for your *junk* sailed
islands and shore, for the Chinese soil,
from which the British departed— left this land,
and handing over with capitalism's prosperity,
people, and parliamentary representation by election
to a transitory state clinging to ideas
of honest campaigns and chosen candidates—
for which the dragon's breath of the Party flames
would nominate approved candidates,
and subjugate true democracy
in this territory of Hong Hong,
to its treatied past.

I hunger with you;
my stomach contracts and growls
as you strike for your beliefs
with the hot acid of digestion;
your body weakens and mind clouds
as days pass by and a world holds its breath
over your predicted demise.

"I cannot breathe" occupies the U.S.mindset;
while I am caught stomaching the wings of ulcerated change,
as time ticks away waiting for you to weaken and die—
hoping your dreams for electoral democracy
(filling young hearts)
are not fading as a mere paragraph
in a university-textbook on broken dreams
to be written and read by those whose thoughts
are controlled by censors
and monitored by Big Brother.

All these fine words;
yet after 108 hours hunger won over your soul;
you ate again as your doctor advised;
the world of free press
chewed on the news of your desire to live,
and again drank in the sweetness of your young Chinese face—
again smiling with future hope,
a voice before the microphones
of the anxious world.

James R. Ellerston
December 6, 2014

Holocaust Commemoration: *Yom Hashoah*

Begin softly in the evening and continue
from sundown tonight until tomorrow's sun sinks,
in remembrance of the six million
killed and perished under the Nazi axis;
In Israel the ten o'clock siren wails
across the world's consciousness—
the two minutes are too brief— people stand at attention
for just this short moment of inaction by thoughtful mourners;
This is a holocaust reminder yearly,
a day by the Jewish calendar of remembrance,
when Ghetto survivors rose up in wartime Warsaw
and fought their captors with illegal guns in starving hands
as their courageous grenades and bottle bombs held evil back.

April 19, 1943 at the gates of the *Juden* Ghetto.
shuttle trucks to the camps were forcibly paused for a while—
that evil might be overcome by righteous cause
before fire bombs fell hellish from a *Luftwaffe* sky;
Those who fought were burned out in blackened plumes,
like those who had meekly surrendered, beaten
when their name and tattooed number were called up—
and forced with brutal treatment to camps and to the eternal gate
to rise up acrid chimneys, bitter fumes of fat-soot smoke
from furnaces or crematorium with emaciated ghetto bodies ablaze;
They were a people walled off and fenced away apart
from the embattled impotent world aflame..

Commemorations involving today's young Israelis raised media complaint
that the expectations of contemporary students were set again too high—
wearing a temporary plastic tattoo for just one day
of five Hollerith digits in clinging plastic film
(numbers of a past IBM system of managed death
obtained from the abuse of ancestral census)
real numerals imposed in remembrance upon white-skinned youthful wrists
and to dial up cell-phone feelings of seventy maybe eighty years back;
But youth had no culture-backed history desiring to hear from real survivors
in this purpled-needling of their university cell-phone skin and texted hearts;

Today's Polish laws against ritual slaughter
make obtaining Kosher meat difficult throughout Europe
(even today making a claim for time on brisk international news
that the mere slicing of an animals throat is deemed too cruel
without the use of a stun-gun before the oven's flame.)

Israeli flags unfurled are carried today by walkers
in pride and patriotic awkwardness moving
on railroad tracks through the gates of Birkenau;
Time changes the telephoto lens
with which history is viewed close or far;
Remember also the other victims please:
gypsies, Polish, homosexuals, Jehovah's Witnesses;
There is an International Roma Day also
held on April 8th each and every year by western calendars—
this year held on the same day with a cycling Jewish calendar.

"*Shema Yisroel*" is a prayer "Keep us safe"
asked as a protection from God over home;
In Brooklyn the torching of the *Mezuzah* parchments
affixed in prayer to doorframes for future hopes defines us:
Such anti-Semitism desecrated these scrolls from modern lintels
and were fire-flamed in vandalism at ten apartment homes
on a day of world-wide solemnity and anguish
for not only those of Jewish faith but those who also weep;
(A neighbor said people of different backgrounds
in the public housing development
needed to make a better effort to get along).

Only when every human animal realizes with certainty
that each of us are animals and also persons,
will they finally confront themselves
and consider joining ranks with other civilized beings;
There is a full responsibility to create remembrance—
not simply pledging "Never again!",
but a committed self to empathy and compassion,
understanding the warning signs,
and invoking prosecution of those guilty of war crimes.
Six million were not killed in battles won or lost
or even as casualties of defensive war,
but "done to death" without any purpose but hatred,
and cruelly bled without regard for humanity or decency
or a single small red-coated child's pain.
Sear humanities meat into our memory
of fire, ash, and smoke yet rising from the oven;
Why think of deadly battles in a Warsaw Ghetto in 1943,
and just yesterday ignore genocide in Rwanda and Sudan?

James R. Ellerston
Apr.8-10, 2013

Bon Voyage Baroness Margaret Thatcher

Now a death on the world stage preparing a military funeral
has reignited debates over forced policies of government involvement
in the history of a strong British woman of resolve;
She helped form the current world , the current Europe;
she will exit from St. Paul's— we now live in her global contributions.

The "Iron Lady" slipped her earthly mooring for her eternal voyage;
today's world leaders rushed condolences to Britain for British loss;
Margaret the Prime Minister changed history for women's roles;
As a polarizing figure in British politics she rolled back the Social State
as the first and only woman Prime Minister in Britain paving women's path.

A stalwart eleven years in office courting Gorbachev and Ronald Reagan;
earned lauds that she didn't just lead the country but "saved the country"
in praises by David Cameron another former P.M. on the BBC;
She took on the union barons mining coal but also strengthened defense
helping to win the Cold War in Europe with open resolve and candor.

She opposed German unification while inviting the eastern bloc outspoken;
leaving a legacy now loved and hated in equal measure with honor and blame
for economic policies worsening the divide between rich and welfare poor;
We may disagree but must respect past achievements and contributions
while she held a post served with dignity, composure, and politicized reserve.

Some news of her passing evoked gasping next to marbles and bronzes—
statues already chiseled of the heroic living; (some welcomed her final death)
Street revelers danced photo placards with red horns held on wooden crosses
twisting tangos drinking champagne in both celebration and mournful loss;
Yet portraits and flowers lean rain-soaked against black iron fences at her London home.

Her final years of declining weakness were portrayed in sympathetic film by Meryl Streep:
Somehow older and fragile she hung on with brittle fortitude in advancing age—
one step alone now taken with the courage of a Falkland War across the sea,
but with the same determination to move or fall that made her politics;
The Falkland Islands recent referendum proclaimed a desire to be British; her victory.

James R. Ellerston
April 9-10, 2013

A Marathon of News

The result of the pressure-cooker blast in Boston sent eight-year-old Martin Richard to his grave;
Medics were pressured for forty-eight in hospital while their lives doctors tried to save.
From pressured television networks there was a news marathon about the current situation;
Pressure running media exploded news to the entire world and to the stunned nation.

The pressure-cooker blast blew at a time to cause the greatest mutilation;
Dead and wounded suffered pressured amputation and lost lives in this abomination;
The pressured male surviving suspect appears to be a self-radicalized Islamic jihadist,
A pressured young naturalized university student, but not a political activist.

It was a pressure-cooker build-up in older brother's misguided plotting mind
Pressure injured two-eighty-two finishing running slower pacing slightly behind;
Pressure of the race day act brought the candle-praying relatives to bended knees,
A shaken pressured President spoke with assurances of justice the nation to appease.

There was a pressure cooking up before the race inside the competing runners all—
The pressure to participate, complete the entire race, and not to trip and fall,
Inner pressure to go the distance, to finish the long set-out course,
Human pressure to better a previous time, to find energy from an inner source.

There was a pressure cooking up inside the brothers to come forth with Islam's jihad position,
A pressure to express one's convictions over some issue without a political coalition;
A pressure to explode onto the world's stage with a statement of protesting anger;
A pressure to risk self as a fugitive, to die or be brought to justice without languor

There was a pressure cooking in the mass media repeatedly to report,
A pressure to keep the news coming with fact from rumor to consistently sort;
A pressure to tell Americans what they hopefully wanted to hear,
A pressure to report the suspects were caught and stop the rampant fear.

In the pressure cooking for police to capture, gunfire exchanged in a Massachusetts town;
In the pressure to find the suspects the metro city had orders to lock down.
In the pressure of locating filmed suspects, one was quickly killed;
A million were pressured to stay inside for a day, as official orders willed.

In the pressure cooking manhunt a woman noticed a ladder out of place;
In the pressure for certainty a helicopter's heat sensors outlined a man but not his face;
In the pressure to hide, a bloodied and battered man was in a driveway-moored trailered boat;
In the pressure to get him to surrender, flash grenades and bullets pierced the hull's painted coat.

There was a pressure cooking in the FBI to find the senseless reason for the acts,
A pressure to extract a confession from the nineteen year-old son and get the tortured facts;
There was a pressure on police to bring in the wounded man alive,
There was a pressure on doctors to treat his wounds and not let his blood pressure dive.

The pressure-cooker for information wanted instant answers at any cost;
A pressure for a tracheotomy opened up the young kid's throat before his life was lost;
Pressured for answers from the crime scene, the young suspect with pen and paper wrote;
In the pressure of the first-aid moment, the runner's shirt given was soon blood soaked.

The pressure-cooker exploding gave an horrific shrapnel blast;
The pressure bomb exploded as straggling runners finishing struggled past;
The pressure behind flying debris killed three outright near the race's end at the flag-draped line,
The pressure bomb wounded 282, some lost a leg— their race time gone with sirens' whine.

The pressure-cooker exploded in historic Boston, a city by the Atlantic sea,
But a pressured nation mourned the violence there, which somehow should never be;
We all feel the pressure of crimes perpetrated by explosives or automatic high powered guns,
But there should be pressure for civilian justice for the father's suspect Muslim sons.

The pressure-cooker exploded, tearing wounds into victims' torso and leg,
Pressure for help and ambulances caused agonized bleeding athletes to beg;
Pressured for quick action, the Islamic father lost his boy by rapid-fire police solution;
Pressured threats of military justice boiled in a democratic nation not looking for absolution.

James R. Ellerston
April 23-26, 2013

history repeating itself

darkened:
cathedral, the Gate, bridges, opera house unlit;
muddled minds, closed minds,
hatred, exclusionism, or closed immigration debates;
abandoned faith, fights protesting religious fervor;
marches against fanatical paraders;
hundreds, thousands, tens of thousands of bigots,
marchers with banners furled,
sewn spider symbols banned on these furling flags;
eighteen thousands in the city once crisped by British bombers
before being curtained in an Iron pen.
all this about folk dress or the native costume cross-culturalism belies
while there live thousands or hundreds in ethnic neighborhoods,
(citizens in the new ghettos of Islamic immigration and monied success);
native citizens question the right of refugees world-over to move next door,
to transplant their feet;
racists would boycott shops, break glass anew.

the clock is turned back to an evil twelve years
by over zealous protection of a gone past,
insistence on the preservation of a life of one language and literature;
there have been generous pleas of a strong democratic woman leader
for Teutonic acceptance of those who would subjugate
their head-covered females.

this time, a forty-one year-old sausage salesmen--
not an artist painter and paper-hanger;
on stage, a mixed race Japanese-Moravian who would lead Czech citizens
into the shadows of an imprisoning abyss;

there is conflict on the streets of Rotterdam;
already twice carpet bombed by the Luftwaffe,
there are protests against tall buildings floored with prayer rugs,
against street signs pointing the direction of Mecca.

some praise the feet-washing of the twelve Apostles,
but damn the self-cleansing before the five-times-daily ritual prayer;
innocently buying a Kabab is seen as financing a head-covering Berka;
the hearts of both sides struggle for perceived rights;
barbed-wire searches for vengeance to fence
while the hoarse fanatics loudly call forth for camps--
and there is an abundant importation of gas from the Russians,
masters of the model of Gulag isolated settlements.

James R. Ellerston
January 6, 2015

while Paris bled freedom

deadly guns splatter across another Nigerian village;
afterward too much fear to remove the expired;
bled-out bodies litter bushes;
another massacre dripping into the African soil,
waiting for a burial of decency in the earth,
or burial in New York on page A8 or A16-- a sorrow.

terror again strikes the world;
more children cower in refugee tents in muddy camps,
while weeping feet plod the endless dusty roads--
hoping for safety and security;
now four thousands of police guard French Jewish schools,
and ten thousands of soldiers try to protect society's daily grind.

we try to protect children's innocence
while television news bleats horror--
news room anchors bask in the spotlights
because there is old news to re-hash;
today something too horrific to show on racist camera
are the thousands of murdered dead in Africa.

more are dying now,
while poets write and you can expression read;
more cartoons will be published by the New Brave in Paris;
writers' pens move across paper pages
to write secure thoughts on typewriters
while Twitter and Youtube are hacked.

classified military-family information
is blatantly published on social media;
poets' anguished words cannot rhyme,
at a time like this-- there is no beauty to behold,
except for world leaders arm in arm in a cloudy Paris street
while decent people only muddle on through troubled days.

silent readers have missed their opportunities
while evil firebombs flew and Lake Chad swimmers drowned;
(such desperate strokes for life in Baga to escape the flames);
wealthy Western tourists believe it will be over by summer,
and the pleasure-life of freedom to travel will be here again--
after hours in security lines while computers grind in passport control.

James R. Ellerston
January 12, 2015

Copenhagen Restaurant February 2015

People are desparate,
they bring flowers in cellophane
what should they do?
pray, kneel, shout in a public microphone?
print a story of pathos in the press?
have a national leader meet the families?
fly flags at half-staff?

There are victims
still grieving,
still mourning,
still feeling indignation.

There is not understanding
when the gunmen are killed
of the question why?

There is not an answer
to hatred.

James R. Ellerston
February 19, 2015

Remembrance Violated

Wild tufts of grasses
trip-up our reverent footsteps
beneath these leafless barren trees
on a hillside isolated under a grey scowl
of cloud tattered sky;
starlings crying out a background requiem.

Here once were two-hundred-fifty deaths
marked with proud standing stone;
rocks of ages past, rocks of lives past,
proudly erected to mark the rite of burial
after a life following the days of feast and ritual,
Jews celebrated in France.

They were a people often set apart
for harassment, torture, murder, crematorium fire;
now five careless teens,
out filled with vile hate—
young muscled bodies striving for something real to do—
have desecrated these chiseled monuments.

Here is carved stone now broken
upon the soil of the cemetery
by hands better in earnest search
of an honest day's toil—
than instead an evening's crime of hate—
now a televised international disgrace.

There have been attacks at a kosher market,
a Copenhagen restaurant, a Belgian museum,
a synagogue-- as the ugly Anti-Semitic disease spreads;
with these desecrated tablets for past loved ones,
we now have an attack against the civilized burial
that defines human life from the animal.

We might even forgive their angst driven minds,
for they might not realize what they really have done;
let us not grieve for these tombs with broken stones,
but mourn for the broken hostility of these five teens--
their strength gone horribly astray--
wrecking havoc on the world's sensibilities.

James R. Ellerston
February 19, 2015

Lame Tank

This is not the Kursk salient caught in a time-lapse lens;
sharp is the contrast of the photographer's picture,
black and white against the snow blown backdrop
and endless flat horizon of the Ukrainian battleground.

The sun is shining in the shadowed colored image;
a burnt-out tank lies useless, careening to one side,
a blackened hulk, its turreted gun lies in a bank of snow,
defining the futility of winter civil war.

Black silhouettes of three men stand,
fighting the cold as much as any enemy;
while they scavenge from the dead carcass
for spare parts to aid another wounded machine.

Armament motionless on the field of past battle,
now made worthless on the endless steppe,
we see the strength of three soldiers to win and survive,
the superiority of willful troops over lame mechanization.

James R. Ellerston
February 19, 2015

Surviving Life

The boy carries all his belongings in a basket,
all that is left of his life without fanfare,
in a dusty site in Alleppo's al-Fardous district;
in the reality of Syria on April 2, 2015.

The boy runs as the haze of background dust fades in perspective
and the empty gurneys can find no whole bodies as burdens;
a barrel bomb was dropped in the continuous senseless fighting.
this is a real picture, no Photoshop, we know this person well.

The boy could have been picking up his laundry
before helping his weary mother carrying her market basket;
she hides the food in the presumed safety of a doorway;
blurred, she is not ready to take the next step for survival.

The boy has youth, determination, stamina, clarity,
and will not be defeated by the blast that changed his life;
he will probably join one side of the battle or another—
and that is nothing to trumpet about.

James R. Ellerston
April 14, 2015

Syrian Refugee in Tears (Yellow Jacket)

"Yellow Jacket" was one of those favorite things
for a child to wear
when they are so young and thin
and happy with life and devoted parents.

It was one of our favorite things for our daughter—
"Yellow Jacket" we called it;
She wore it in the motorboat at the lake,
wore it on the first day of kindergarten
in the photograph my wife took
on the front step of the house
on her first day of school
(at least my sixty-five year old memory
remembers it that way
if it wasn't so in fact).

"Yellow Jacket" was one of those favorite things
for a child to wear
when they are so young and thin
and happy with life and devoted parents.

We found it years later when cleaning the attic—
much to small for her to wear anymore;
I can't remember if we discarded it
in its aged molded state
or kept it in hopes it would clean up
and that a grandchild would wear it—
bringing back memories of our daughter's childhood—
or our own youth
when our hair was naturedly colored;
I hope we were able to keep it.

"Yellow Jacket" was one of those favorite things
for a child to wear
when they are so young and thin
and happy with life and devoted parents.

The colored painful photo
came across the internet Reuters news waves—
here was the young Syrian girl
in her own "Yellow Jacket"
and the Syrian girl in all her innocence was in tears—
the girl had survived a ground-to-ground missile attack
her home in Aleppo's Bab al-Hedeed district on April seventh
lost its feeling of safety, and she clutched the hand of a friend—
like so many mornings of my daughter's insecurity
from being hurried too much on the way to school or daycare;
She would return from a day feeling safe in the evening—
when we had more time and patience,
and she was intelligent enough
to know that Dad would be home for the evening
if he lit a fire in the fireplace.

"Yellow Jacket" was one of those favorite things
for a child to wear
when they are so young and thin
and happy with life and devoted parents.

So much pain can exist dressed in a yellow jacket,
pain avoidable, caused then and now.

James R. Ellerston
April 12, 2015

In A Sentimental Mood (A Letter to Home)

Fog surrounds the variously worded lyrics, and history of our song;
men from Missouri flat-bottom boats, to clipper ship hands seaward sailing.
all sang "Oh, Shenandoah" as a shanty raising anchor or winded sails;
today's anthem reflects aching personal nostalgia for place and time.

Sung by our choir in a'cappella voice it draws out raw emotion
from the audience by the vocal beauty of disciplined youth,
no raspy Bob Dylan voice in folksingers playback on a scratchy LP.
but smooth voices raising praise of melody and poetry soul ward.

With bands of surviving veterans 'Johnny' came home from the Civil War;
arriving home with many variants, full bodied, marching healthy and strong,
or after specific instruments might have delicately amputated crutched limbs;
rampant vicious disease may have taken toll even over the battles victors.

Dancers in swinging skirts sway next to black tuxedos;
even the hair styles are groomed for the period; my throat chokes;
the image is striking, costumes suspended in time, my eyes water;
an audience hears the sounds and melodies of a bygone era.

In front of my eyes I see a vision of the Hamburg Swing Kids,
their love of the music, motion, dance, and social circle swirling,
before being loaded on the trucks, hauled away by the Nazis,
taken to the Camps and killed for their love of outlawed music and life.

Swing Kids danced to a different drummer than the Hitler Youth,
and they loved the imported 78rpm records from America that were
secreted into Germany and so prized by the youth denied their radios;
denied the broadcasts of the Glenn Miller Band to the American forces.

When Paris was freed, Major Miller would want to fly to Paris,
to broadcast his morale boosting music further into Europe
than the bunker broadcasts from London reaching the downtrodden;
his plane lumbered crossing the Channel but never reached France.

The band's promised broadcasts went ahead with out their leader;
on a Christmas morning 1944 loss of Miller's plane was announced
over the network radio waves to the anguish of millions of fans;
decades later further radar analysis revealed the downing by friendly fire.

Performers keep alive the traditions of the 40's Swing Era,
the great Dance Orchestras that entertained the troops and those battling
the ration cards and shortages at home from Britain to Iowa;
sounds, songs, melodies, styles of clothes and movements of dance.

The Allied forces had one weapon the enemy didn't have—
Glenn Miller, who even broadcast shows into Germany to win their minds;
now keeping the authentic sound of this era alive connects us to a time
when music as motivation and a thread with home kept men fighting on.

James R. Ellerston
April 21, 2015

earthquake aftermath April 27th

while the German dogs continue to sniff fallen bricks and stones
my body lies resting on the pavement outside the overburdened hospital—
one of a million children subjected to the shaking earth and resultant destruction
in my home country of high mountains on the border between India and China;
it is Monday, a start of my new life, after the ground shook on Saturday;
I am thankful for the bandage on my hand where the I.V. enters painfully.

smoking fires fog the air as bodies of the dead are cremated as they are found;
soldiers continue to load the few helicopters to take the injured to help;
the beds and hallways still standing are full of the severely injured;
my head bandaged, the medicine continues to drip life into me as I sleep—
I am one of the lucky children who has been found and treated;
I am thankful for the bandage on my hand where the I.V. enters painfully.

while my country suffers in helpless pain, death and loss,
the most wealthy country on the planet is intent on burning down its cities,
fighting each other in the streets, destroying buildings over suspended racism—
this evil plagues the Americans when any excuse surfaces like now in Baltimore;
while their fires burn unnecessarily, I lie on cold concrete in Dhading Besi, Nepal;
I am thankful for the bandage on my hand where the I.V. enters painfully.

James R. Ellerston
April 28, 2015

(Praying for) Safe Passage

two women peer through the dust,
the storm of sand in Allahabad
on the banks of the river Ganges
in another day of dry wind in India.

flowing garments of yellow, orange, purple,
such bright fabrics whip in air blown dusty patterns
across forward leaning stern bodies within the white background;
cautious hands shield mouths and noses from flying particles.

dusty shoes are white from intention or passage through the drifts;
nothing is visible in the faceless photo except the colors of two flapping
silk-dressed persons balancing themselves as if in a blizzard background;
waves of flowing holy water lap at the determined faithful on the bank.

James R. Ellerston
May 12, 2015

A.M.E Church in Charleston Founded 1816

they went to church praying;
the Lord did not shield them from earthly harm
when the gunman opened fire
in Charleston where personal hatred
challenged forgiveness of sin;
where a gun was given as a birthday gift;
where premeditation triumphed over penitence,
where a demented racist mind
quick ushered nine into the eternal promise of life
too soon for comprehension.

James R. Ellerston
June 18, 2015

British Massacred on a Tunisian Beach

Like bad money, the sprayed bullets
drove $515 million tourist dollars ($US)
from the economy of the north-African state;
its Mediterranean shores left waxed naked;
cocktail glasses under beach umbrellas unfilled,
pink plastic umbrellas and stirrer sticks unused—
as the ice melted between strangers left in a scene of horror.

Sunbathers from their chaise loungers of toweled sunburned sand
are headed for final caskets and crematorium;
other bikinis are traded for golden aircraft tickets of evacuation,
as for some, the promise of a heavenly healthy vacation
was traded for an entrance at the decisive airport gate to Manchester—
to an eternal PTSD fear whenever guns are fired
or simple firecracker celebration heard.

Children everywhere with a sandman between their toes
are tucked into bed with a new worldwide appreciation
and parental reluctance to leave home and hearth
for even amusement entertainment at seaside Bristol;
new travel brochures look like printed enamel paper script
bearing risk and fear in Kodak colors without any value,
or in consumers' pockets no future travel dreams.

James R. Ellerston
June 30, 2015

Obituary (died July 1, 2015)

Briton Sir Nicholas Winton yesterday died;
for a while he kept a secret even from his wife
who later found his scrapbook documentation
of providing salvation for the 669--
the Czech children of the Kindertransport
on trains organized so skillfully
which steamed through Nazi Germany

When he was twenty-nine years old,
he was in young manhood and had vision,
and the Blitzkrieg War had not yet started in 1939;
later recognized and knighted
he was rewarded with a long life itself--
living one hundred six years with dignity and worth:
the savior of children given a chance to survive--
alone his trains of love rolled West
before brutal death steamed East.

His soul has flown up against simple daily needs wind,
rising inspiration beyond what ordinary mortals
might be tempted to even dream--
but many parents believed as they said goodbye
and with courage hung the numbered card about their child's neck,
and the whistle blew
and tears of gratitude flowed
for the open arms at the end of the ride.

James R. Ellerston
July 2, 2015

New Hellenistic History Waits Another Day; Windmills Turn On

An aged sun brown sinewed arm of a Greek pensioner anguished
pounded on the security door of the closed bank
in hope, desperation, frustration--
out of funds to pay rent, electricity, and buy food;
there was no immediate promise of money,
only cutbacks and national austerity.

The gray-haired woman stood in the sun,
waited on the sidewalk for several hours;
she collapsed and a National Bank employee
(barred from offering Euro currency at the teller's window)
rushed around from a benevolent door,
and offered only bottled water to her waning body and parched lips.

Affluent tourists continue to crowd the picturesque islands
from the ATM-driven cruise ships plying the Aegean Sea,
the outdoor cafes full of their hunger for sun-bronzed history;
ragged pillars and the raided archaeology of former conquests
now diminish the copied statues of awe and adulation;
this seat of world democracy has hopes on imposed VAT taxes--
marring blue skies, green seas, and hopes of a white-washed future.

Like all families worldwide struggling with debt, hoping for future times
better than the present, living with creditors payments and interest charges,
the government of this war-torn, border-rearranged nation,
once proud, now struggling with external financial dictats
as solutions to their borrowing in the international family,
now subject to debt, poverty and foreign imposed shame--
all this leads to ambition for territories of others,
to threatening persecuting behavior at blamed targets--
all now politicized with the new dangerous raising of Right arms in salute.

James R. Ellerston July 7, 2015

Koran on the Battlefield

His hand is large, between thumb and finger strongly
he grasps a richly decorated thick volume of the Koran
as he walks the war-torn streets of Damascus--
a Free Syrian fighter in the city district of Jobar.

Wreckage and carnage surround the young man,
back slung down with the weight of automatic weapons
over a navy short sleeved shirt from any American golf course
and camouflaged fatigue pants, wide leather belt.

Photographer skill caught the back of his black curly hair, beard,
left arm. slim wrist and hand, white skin on the back of his neck;
we know little about him but his dedication to a cause
he believes is true to him at this time.

An evident purposeful nature to his stride
gives away both his strength and youth;
in the Muslim world he could be any slim-hipped boy next door
(or transported from any affluent American suburb).

James R. Ellerston
July 8, 2015
Reuters photographer Bassdem Khableh July 6, 2015

Monument to Bones

twenty years later
she searches with a stick in the woods,
hunting for a trace of her son's bones--
the spot where he was last seen, lay wounded;
evidence to prove in courts that he once breathed and lived.

twenty years later
135 from the mass grave lost so quickly
will be buried today; identified--
DNA is a slow process from a genocide,
when 8000 boys and men were killed.

twenty years later
pictures of boys and men
hang in honor upon apartment walls--
above carpets and two decades of tears
covering the floors on which sons and husbands trod.

twenty years later
women and men weep over those identified,
skeletal remains to be again interred--
this time with individual coffins, markers
in a memorial center in Polocari.

twenty years later
the Muslim families of Srebrenica cannot forget
this massacre in Bosnia and Herzegovina by Christians--
when Orthodox and Catholic forces killed their beloved on July 11th, 1995,
and haven't yet paid penitence for that for which there is no absolution

written this July 11, 2015   James R. Ellerston

A Brief Commentary on Marriage

This spring Omar Shariff, aka Doctor Zhivago
passed away after immortalizing himself in David Lean's 1967 film;
Unlike the more recent BBC film for television, more fast paced--
in Lean's film it is the three second cameo shot in a lumbering freight car
moving across the Russian steppe that has remained in my mind
to symbolize the enduring love of marriage.

In the straw in the bottom of the train car
lay an elderly couple, grey haired,
arms embraced around each other,
lips briefly touching in the manner of an enduring marriage—
continuing to make the best of the time
they still have together.

Uri Zhivago, a poet, gazes out a ventilation port,
and the director's camera gazed at a silvery full moon
in search of beauty,
but the real beauty was the image of the couple—
in the straw, still in love with each other's aging bodies,
making the most of the moment in three seconds of film.

The uncertainties of their future situation,
uncertainties of their future destination,
the horrors of that historical time as we know it meant little,
as the couple was escaping to a new life together;
Their only certainty was that they had each other to love;
such courage a life partner gives.

James R. Ellerston
June 4, September 17, 2015

at the borders September 2015

a razor-wire curtain has descended over Europe;
efforts to manage the refugee crisis
are stopping the tired, the poor
at border crossings across the nations.

those who have survived the sea crossing or walk
are now stopped at the Hungarian border,
borders of Serbia and Croatia—
the border with Germany.

nations all too familiar with closed borders
from the iron grip of past guarded walls
which kept them from freedom, prosperity,
and free travel, are stopping others now.

new walls raise their ugly posts, wire, concrete,
to block hopeful parents with babies in their arms;
stopping people yearning to be free, safe--
the tempest-tossed of warfare further south.

James R. Ellerston
September 14, 2015

Timeless Weaponry Toward Israel

Is he poised for a David statue for our time?
one might easily call the young Palestinian
armed with rock and spinning sling—
a subject worthy of sculpture by a modern Michelangelo.

Dressed in shirtless defined torso,
young manhood's developed body shadowed by burning sun,
muscled arm with pouch spun out just before deadly throw—
he practices the graceful dance of ancient attack.

Legs in jeans with blue uniform legs twisted and creased,
leather belted tightly around defined slim waist,
natural anatomy of the feet balanced on agile toes—
close detailing narrow treads of heel-elevated white athletics.

Raised in graceful poise, a body armed in motion strong;
beautiful, timeless, as the millenniums attack or defense;
a young man hurls a stone towards a hated enemy—
posed physique, ageless as sculpted warfare in Goliath's time.

James R. Ellerston
October 6th, 11, 2015

Dreams Under Head and Pillow

The tired young teen sprawls across his bed,
barefooted, shirtless, legs jack-knifed upon a dusty mattress;
upon the floor he lies dangerously close
to the bombed-away rubble of the room's edge.

He sleeps insecurely since the July 2014 destruction
of his Gaza neighborhood left naked beams of concrete
standing for blocks of apartments desecrated,
no longer clothed in shrouding mortar.

With no where else to go he sleeps what is left of his youth away
next to twisted reinforcing jagged steel
with the little comfort and familiarity his bed
in the corner of his destroyed family's apartment can bring.

After the brutal Israeli attacks
this open-air sleeping refuge provides the nest
orphaned lost childhood bitter needs
to overcome another day of hatred and flag-clutching dreams.

James R. Ellerston
October 9, 2015

Natural or Synthetic Postludes

There is fear, there are tears;
a child clutches their father's gripping hand
walking, half wading, half paddling with stiffened legs—
seeking the shore, the bank, the beach, the boundary.

Fearing, trusting, hoping, believing;
numb, cold, shivering, chilled, teeth chattering;
today, tomorrow, in a week, month, next year—
a plan, a distance, a way, a hike, a boat, ride a train.

An immediate journey is over;
the clammy bodies are in open air;
a chance, generous, welcoming hand has only the first mission—
when shock, hypothermia, and exposure might win out.

In the few precious minutes that can make that difference
between life and death it can be quickly handed out
after a swim ashore, a climb on the beaches, sheltering in grass—
beside the sea, the road, the stream, the wire-fence, where gathered.

With the border open and the basic gift of warmth
now there is hope for the child;
the father's strength returns and—
the mother's breast starts to make milk again.

Invaluable gift, a silver flexible sheet at this time;
they huddle beneath it, wind rattles it, rain is held off;
parents gather it around the child—
feel the hope of warmth retained and thanksgiving.

Among options are goat hair, sheep's wool, synthetic polar-fleece,
or the rattle of space-age compact Mylar folded in small pouches;
blankets are as old as gathering hide, spinning and weaving fiber—
or as new as those made by the mile from today's chemicals.

Shapes and uses of fabrics can be the woven art of a culture,
and basic gift by those to give who have more than they need,
to those who have left or lost everything behind—
and somehow must begin their lives and homes anew.

It is an immediate responsibility to provide survivable blankets
when the simplest portable gift of warmth and shelter
might mean the continuity of life itself, a glimmer of love—
for those forced to traverse the distance and survive the storm.

James R. Ellerston
October 11, 2015

Final Exaltation for Veteran Strachan

brisk wind sweeps across fallow fields flying drying leaves;
strains of century's verse comforting mournful troubled souls;
bugles sounding echoed Taps' respect for veteran (s) (Strachan's) last lost dawn;
years of family friends, strong vocal song—
now passed from time forever gone.

oil canvas painted for infants' joyful colors; yes, wives and mothers loved;
a life has passed, decades spent, in affection for his family's blood;
strong harvesters have gleaned good grain from these sturdy parental stalks,
growing seasons fed, refreshed, and nourished—
(Sean's) (child's) blond-haired locks.

his military service guarded the home front from harmful snare for nation's peace,
taking younger years, yeah, a gift of patriotism's belief;
respect for rank and saluting guns draw us today around a flag-draped box;
dedicate the trumpeters' song over soil's bountiful blossoms—
a grave for past toils' brown now withered leaf.

for burial of Veteran Richard Strachan,   October 25, 2015
James R. Ellerston
October 24, 2015

CHECK OUT JIM'S OTHER BOOKS!

Available for purchase at Amazon.com

Like People, These Are Not Meant To Stand Alone

James Ray Ellerston

CHECK OUT JIM'S OTHER BOOKS!

Available for purchase at Amazon.com

CHECK OUT JIM'S OTHER BOOKS!

Available for purchase at Amazon.com

Poems From
Travels In Three
Countries

James Ray Ellerston

Book Publishing and Cover Design
By Keegan Joël VanDevender

Keegan Joël VanDevender attended Oskaloosa Community Schools having interests in Biology, Chemistry, English, Spanish and French. In 2010, Keegan decided to take his interest in the Spanish language to the next level by studying in Quetzaltenango (Xela), Guatemala. Upon returning to the United States, Keegan had a strong urge to learn another language, therefore, he looked into other abroad programs. In 2012, Keegan left the States to spend 11.5 months in French- Speaking (Wallonia), Belgium. While in Europe, he was able to travel to many countries including France, the Netherlands, Luxembourg, Germany, and Spain. After his time in Belgium, Keegan returned to the United States to Study Biology, Spanish and French.

Keegan is currently taking classes in the pursuit of a degree in nursing. He plans to earn a masters of science in nursing, in order to become a nurse practitioner.